The Art of Estate Planning

CHERYL CHAPMAN HENDERSON

Copyright © 2020 by Cheryl Chapman Henderson

ISBN: 9798666784549

All rights reserved. This book or any portion thereof may not be reproduced or used in any manner whatsoever without the express written permission of the publisher except for the use of brief quotations in a book review.

DEDICATION

This book is dedicated to my husband, Lonnie P. Henderson, who has labored as much as I in getting it published and to my father, Clinton W. Chapman, who encouraged and always made room for us to think, read, and explore.

DISCLAIMER & WARNINGS

This book is intended to provide general information and is not intended as legal advice or a substitute for legal counsel. The author has written this book to address the general, everyday estate planning needs of most Americans. However, the book makes no attempt to address gift and estate tax concepts, income tax specifics, business planning, dynasty planning, or state-specific laws.

References to laws and legal principles are those that were in effect at the time this book went to print. As laws are continually changing, the writer is not liable in the event that laws have changed since the book's publication.

Unless otherwise referenced, all definitions are from *Webster's New World Dictionary of the American Language* (2nd ed. 1972).

The names used in examples are entirely fictitious.

CONTENTS

ACKNOWLEDGEMENTS ix
LIST OF ABBREVIATIONS xi
INTRODUCTION 1
PART I – THE ART OF ESTATE PLANNING FUNDAMENTALS 3
   Your Authority to Have Your Plan Enforced 3
   Capacity, Incapacity, and Guardianships 9
      Legal Incapacity and Guardianships 10
   Steps to Moving Forward in the Art of Estate Planning... 17
      1.   Commit to Taking Action Now 18
      2.   Prepare Yourself by Considering Three Things 19
      3.   Identify the right estate planning attorney for you ... 22
   The Art of Estate Planning Is a Process 23
PART II – THE 7 ESSENTIAL ESTATE PLANNING TOOLS 37
   Above Ground Tools 39
      Tool 1 – Powers of Attorney 40
         Powers of Attorney (POA) for Finances and Personal
         Decisions 40
            Fundamentals 42
            Agents 43
            Types of POAs 45
            Practical Considerations 47

Health Care Powers of Attorney (HCPOA) 50

Tool 2 – Advance Directives and Advance Care Plans . 52

    Advance Directives for Healthcare Decisions 52

    Advance Care Plans (ACPs) 54

Tool 3 – HIPAA Authorizations 58

Below Ground Tools 61

Tool 4 – Wills and Probate 62

    Wills 62

    Probate 67

    Why Not Probate for Asset Transfers? 73

Tool 5 – Joint Ownership 77

    Advantages of Joint Ownership 77

    Disadvantages of Joint Ownership 79

Tool 6 – Transfers by Beneficiary Designations 86

    Advantages of Beneficiary Designations 86

Additional Tools 90

    Outright Gifts 90

    Life Estate Deeds 92

A Little-Known Truth 95

Tool 7 – Trusts 98

    Trust Components 100

    Types of Trusts and Features 102

What You Can Do with Trusts: Essential Planning Solutions.. 106

What You Can do with Trusts: Beyond the Essentials.... 115

PART III - FINISHING TOUCHES 125

Importance of Good Counsel.. 125

A Word on Digital Assets 131

Leaving Access to Your Information................................. 134

Personal Private Information Profile............................ 136

FINAL THOUGHTS 138

ABOUT THE AUTHOR.. 140

INDEX... 142

ACKNOWLEDGEMENTS

This book is the culmination of more than 30 years of estate planning experience. I want to first thank and honor God, who gave me the vision to write this book and has been with me every step of the way.

I thank my husband, Lonnie P. Henderson, my spiritual compass, who has encouraged me to stay on course.

Next, I thank my dad, Clinton W. Chapman, who was my inspiration for becoming a lawyer and has modeled for me what it means to be an "attorney and counselor at law."

I thank my family for their encouragement and support, especially my son Caliph Johnson.

I am deeply grateful for the hundreds of clients who have invited me into their lives and allowed me to guide them as they planned their estates.

I thank the magnificent team that has supported me, and special thanks, Katherine Bell, for your untiring support and contributions over the years.

I am also grateful for all those who have invited me to speak with their congregations, organizations, family, and friends.

Thanks to Dave Zampano and Phil Miner for helping me to understand the importance of Advance Care Planning for our clients.

Much appreciation goes to my professional colleagues who have shared their experiences, wisdom, and knowledge, and to Richard Schmitt, who has taken the time to review this book before publication and provide his invaluable and encouraging feedback. Thanks also to my colleagues Michael Gross and Michelle Lanchester, who provided valuable feedback on real estate and guardianship matters. To those final proof sets of eyes, thank you, Marcy Moore, my husband Lonnie P. Henderson, and my colleague Peg Shaw.

And finally, I thank my editors, especially my talented and supportive sister, Clarissa Chapman Bowie, who through her editing has taught me how to become a better writer. Getting from manuscript to published book is an art in and of itself. Terri Whitmire and the amazing team at Writer's Tablet Agency have navigated me through this phase with good counsel, editing, creativity, and exceptional knowledge of how things work. The entire publishing process was handled with professionalism and ease.

LIST OF ABBREVIATIONS

ACP	Advance Care Planning
AD	Advance Directive
DAPTs	Domestic Asset Protection Trusts
HCPOA	Healthcare Power of Attorney
HIPAA	Health Insurance Portability and Accountability Act
ILITs	Irrevocable Life Insurance Trusts
IRA	Individual Retirement Account
IRS	Internal Revenue Service
POA	Power of Attorney
POD	Payable on Death
SRT	Standalone Retirement Trust
SSI	Supplemental Security Income
TbyE	Tenants by the Entirety
TOD	Transfer on Death
TODD	Transfer on Death Deed

INTRODUCTION

Art refers to the human ability to make things or execute a plan.

A plan is a detailed method formulated beforehand for doing something.

Estate is all the property, possessions and capital owned by someone.

The art of estate planning is your ability to make and execute a detailed plan — formulated beforehand — for dealing with your property, possessions, and capital. Your most important capital is YOU and your ability to make decisions.

Estate planning brings together many facets of your life. It also interconnects with many different legal disciplines. Good estate planning is not a rote, paint-by-numbers, fill-in-the-blanks, or off-the-shelf process. Each plan, if properly approached, is unique. That's what makes estate planning an art.

Whether you are new to estate planning or renewing your existing plan, my desire is that you will find this book a handy guide to the art of estate planning.

You can expect to learn:

- The keys to success in estate planning, which start with your authority as an estate planner.
- What your authority means in estate planning.
- The consequences of legal incapacity and guardianships.
- The making of a good estate plan.
- The importance of good legal counsel and how to select one.
- The number one hindrance to estate planning and how to overcome it.
- What to expect when you go through the estate planning process.
- The seven essential tools of estate planning: powers of attorney, advance directives, HIPAA Authorizations, Wills, Joint Ownership, Transfers on Death, and Trusts.
- How the estate planning tools work and what to consider when using them.
- A little-known truth about the most popular estate planning tools. It's a secret that few talk about.
- Trusts and how they work.
- Additional estate planning tools you should know about.
- Advanced planning techniques to be aware of.

The art of estate planning begins and ends with you, so let's begin learning the art.

PART I – THE ART OF ESTATE PLANNING FUNDAMENTALS

YOUR AUTHORITY TO HAVE YOUR PLAN ENFORCED

One morning, my husband Lonnie and I were headed toward the office on the Capital Beltway during the height of rush-hour traffic. There are usually four lanes of heavily congested traffic in each direction. While traveling that morning, we noticed something very odd – there was no oncoming traffic. There was not a single car on the four-lane stretch as far as the eye could see. As we continued, we saw an amazing sight. All four lanes of traffic that should have been coming towards us were stopped. In front of the vehicles stood a lone state trooper astride his motorcycle with *his back to the traffic.*

Authority is the power or right to give orders, make decisions, and enforce obedience

By his authority and not by his physical force, this state trooper commanded the rush-hour traffic to stop. His authority was backed by the State of Maryland as evidenced by his badge and uniform. He was so confident in his authority that he was poised with his back to the traffic.

The same confidence and poise displayed by the state trooper can be yours in planning your estate. You have the authority to make decisions, give orders, and enforce obedience. In fact, you have God-given authority over most areas of your life. And, under our legal system, your authority to make enforceable decisions about yourself and your assets is ample.

For the past several years, I have been teaching a workshop entitled "Your Authority, Your Control, Your Estate Plan." I believe that most of us do not know the extent of our estate planning authority. The message is this: you have the ability to develop a plan that is appropriate for you and your loved ones. It is a plan that carries out your express directions, and one you can rely on as legally enforceable even if you lose capacity and after you die. This is your estate planning authority.

You can develop a plan that results in confidence and peace of mind. How? Here are three keys to your success:

- o **Key 1:** Know your authority. Your authority is broad. Most of you do not know the breadth of your authority in making estate planning decisions. With good counsel, you can explore the limits of your estate planning authority.

- **Key 2:** Exercise your authority by making good estate planning decisions. You will examine the concepts and tools that will enable you to make the right decisions. With good counsel, you will be guided in the best planning options.

- **Key 3:** Put your decisions in writing. Having binding written decisions is the third key to legally enforceable estate plans. Your written documents are like the state trooper's badge and uniform. Those seeing your legally sound documents are obliged to operate in obedience.

So, what is good estate planning? What kinds of decisions should you be making? We will be examining these questions in the next chapter and throughout this book. However, before moving on, I want to leave you with this thought: you have the authority to make decisions over most areas of your life. If you apply the three keys — knowing your authority, making the right decisions, and expressing them correctly — you can be assured of success in your overall life.

Keys to success in estate planning:

Knowing your authority.

Exercising your authority by good estate planning decisions.

Putting your decisions in the right written form.

NUGGET

The same success keys can be applied to every other area of your life:

Knowing your authority.

Exercising your authority by making the right decisions.

WHAT IS GOOD ESTATE PLANNING?

You have the authority, with few exceptions, to accomplish whatever you want when it comes to estate planning. You can best exercise your authority by making good estate planning decisions. Let's look at what good estate planning is.

Most of us want to assert as much control over our sphere of living as possible. Specifically, most of us want to stay in control over our ability to make decisions and over our resources. Is that you? Read on.

Consider this: good estate planning allows you to maintain control over *you and your assets*, even if you become incapacitated or upon death. Borrowing from Esperti and Peterson's work, *Loving Trust*[1], here is a working definition of good estate planning:

1. You transfer your decision-making authority if you become incapacitated or disabled. That means that you determine who makes life decisions for you and how those decisions will be made.

---

[1] Robert A. Esperti and Renno L. Peterson, Loving Trust: How to Provide for Yourself and Guarantee the Future of Your Loved Ones (Viking Adult, 1988).

2. When you die, you determine who gets your assets, when they get them, how they get them, and why they get them.

3. Whether it's incapacity or death, you formulate a plan that minimizes taxes, expenses, delays, pain, and mess.

Good estate planning involves a plan that transfers your decision-making authority along with your instructions in the event of incapacity and that transfers your assets upon death to whom you want, when you want, how you want, and why you want, all while minimizing taxes, expenses, delays, pain, and mess to you and your loved ones.

In the business world, succession planning ensures that the business is not interrupted and continues to operate smoothly after the death or disability of its owner. A business succession plan is designed to perpetuate the life of the business.

You have a responsibility to ensure that your loved ones' well-being is not interrupted by your incapacity or death so that the business of living can continue. Regard good estate planning as your personal succession plan.

Capacity, Incapacity, and Guardianships

You have authority to make your estate planning decisions because of your legal capacity.

Capacity is the ability to do something.

Legal capacity encompasses your authority to make competent decisions about yourself and your property and finances. Every adult is presumed to have legal capacity unless otherwise determined.

Mr. White, a retiree, developed sudden onset dementia. By the time his son and only child recognized his condition, Mr. White was completely unable to make decisions for himself. He needed 24-hour care and supervision. His son brought his father to live with him and hired a full-time caregiver. His son's financial outlay was staggeringly high despite the fact that Mr. White received enough income to cover the cost of his care. Because Mr. White's son had neither a power of attorney nor access to his father's bank account, a guardianship proceeding was necessary to pay bills and to make legal decisions on his father's behalf. The outcome of the proceeding was that Mr. White was declared legally incapacitated and his son was appointed his legal guardian and given access to his bank account, but only after five months, the involvement of three attorneys and two healthcare professionals and a cost of $12,000.

Legal Incapacity and Guardianships

Legal incapacity is the exception to your inherent authority to make estate planning decisions. If you do not possess the capacity to make decisions for yourself either in the short term or indefinitely, your authority to act is null and void. You may not possess capacity for a variety of reasons, such as illness, disease, trauma, injury, mental health issues, drugs, or substance misuse. Unless there is an agent appointed under a valid power of attorney, the only way legal decisions can be made for you is through the court appointment of a legal guardian.

A minor does not possess capacity for making legal decisions or to manage property. The parent is the *natural* guardian who makes legal decisions for the child until adulthood – age 18 or 21, depending on the state; however, legal guardianship is required if the minor has no parent to make decisions. An adult may have never possessed the capacity to make competent decisions because of injury or disease during birth or childhood, and a legal guardian must be appointed.

Guardianship is based on the concept of legal incapacity. It's important not to confuse legal incapacity with disability. An adult is presumed by law to be capable of making his or her own decisions. A person may be disabled without losing the capacity for making his or her own decisions; for example, a person totally paralyzed from quadriplegia may still have the ability to make sound decisions.

Here are some things to know about legal incapacity and guardianship:

- **You Come Under Court Control.** If you do not have a plan and your legal capacity is questioned or a professional has determined that you are legally incapacitated, then you are likely to be forced into guardianship proceedings. If the court decides that you lack capacity to manage your affairs, then you become a ward of the state. The court will appoint a guardian to make decisions for you or for your property or both. In some states, the person who manages your property is known as the conservator.

- **You May Lose Your Freedom of Choice.** As a ward under guardianship, you may be stripped of all authority to make legal decisions for yourself and to manage and control your property. Your guardian's authority to make decisions for you can be all encompassing. For example, you may lose your freedom to associate with whom you want, to decide where you live, to travel, to make your own healthcare decisions, or to choose your healthcare provider. Your guardian makes those decisions for you. The guardian (or conservator) of your property will take control of your property, make purchases for you, pay your bills, decide what you own, make your investment decisions, and manage your spending. The guardian can even sell your home to pay the guardian's fees and expenses. Whether you have a personal guardian or a guardian of your property, you lose your freedom and the right to make your own choices.

- **The Court Selects Your Guardian.** The choice of guardian is made by the court. While the court tends to favor family members or people you have selected in your power of attorney, the court may bypass them because of family dynamics and legal requirements and will appoint a disinterested person, usually a lawyer or professional guardian.

- **Guardianship Is Costly.** The initial process of establishing guardianship can cost you thousands of dollars. As with most legal proceedings, costs escalate if there are contentions or controversies; however, unlike most legal proceedings, the guardianship continues indefinitely along with ongoing fees and expenses. Once under guardianship, your estate will be responsible for guardianship fees, court costs, and other expenses.

- **Guardianships Are Open to the Public.** The determination that you are legally incapacitated and under guardianship is public record and can be found by anyone who chooses to search. You lose your privacy.

- **Your Spouse's Rights Are Also Affected.** The intimacy of marriage is affected by guardianship, especially if someone other than your spouse is appointed guardian. Your spouse may lose the right to make decisions customarily made inside the marriage. The guardian of property can interfere with the rights of the spouse to use, enjoy, and control joint property and property used in the marriage. The guardian can even separate spouses.

- **Guardianship Often Lasts Until Your Death.** It is rare that a person under adult guardianship recovers her authority from the court to make her own decisions despite efforts to do so. Most guardianships terminate only when the incapacitated person dies.

- **Older Adults Are at Greater Risk for Guardianship.** Injury and disease (especially dementia) can lead to loss of capacity. Loss of capacity disproportionately affects older adults, who are more likely to encounter guardianship proceedings.

- **Guardianship Is Usually Required to Manage Inheritances Left to Minor Children.** Since a minor is legally prevented from managing finances or property, guardianship is required to manage the child's inheritance until the child reaches legal age. At legal age, the child receives the entire inheritance with no binding safeguards. Imagine the disastrous consequences of handing over thousands of dollars to an 18-year-old! You should never leave money or other major assets directly to a minor.

- **Guardianship Is Living Probate.** At death, the probate court appoints a representative to make decisions on your behalf, including decisions about your property if you had not made other arrangements. This is called "death probate," which is discussed in a subsequent chapter. Guardianship is sometimes referred to as "living probate." Like death probate, the representative or guardian is appointed to make decisions about you and your personhood and about your property while you are still living. While many estate plans are designed to avoid probate at death; not enough plans are designed to avoid probate while living. There are more reasons to avoid living probate than to avoid probate at death.

- **Most Guardianships Can Be Avoided by Proper and Timely Planning.** A properly prepared and maintained power of attorney is the key planning tool to prevent or minimize guardianships. A trust along with a power of attorney provides an even greater safeguard against guardianship.

- **The Role of Guardianship for Adults.** Adult guardianship is an essential tool for those adults who have no one else to handle their affairs. It is designed to protect frail, elderly, and vulnerable adults from abuse, neglect, and exploitation. However, apart from these circumstances, you should consider adult guardianships as a last resort.

Success in estate planning involves exercising your authority to make decisions even if you later lose the capacity to decide. The good news is that even if you lose legal capacity, if you have an estate plan you won't lose control. Your agent can be empowered to make decisions for you as you would want them made.

Not enough planning is designed to avoid living probate.

Steps to Moving Forward in the Art of Estate Planning

Why do 70% of Americans not have wills? Why do an even greater number not have powers of attorney? Procrastination! Of the top financial issues people postpone, estate planning ranks number two!

Most plans fail because either there are no plans in place, or once in place, they are not kept up-to-date. We all know, either from personal experience or from news reports, the pain and mess created when someone fails to plan.

My goal is to help you move forward in planning your estate. Consider this: the greatest obstacle to moving forward in estate planning is inertia. Inertia is the human tendency to resist moving forward or taking action. It is the tendency to remain stuck in a fixed position. We have all experienced inertia in some areas of our lives. Based on the statistics and personal experiences, we know that estate planning is an area where inertia abounds!

The origin of the word "inertia" reveals the key to why we stay stuck in the first place. Inertia comes from the Latin word meaning *lack of skill or art*. Aha! Many of us stay stuck because we don't know what to do or how to do it. We simply lack the art or skill, and we don't know how to get started. Is that you? If so, then below are three strategies for overcoming inertia.

1. Commit to Taking Action Now

Making a commitment to take action is the first step. I continually remind my clients and the many people I encounter that <u>now</u> is the time to pursue estate planning. Now is when you have the capacity to make sound decisions. Now is the time your field of vision is the widest. Now is the time to put your plan in writing. Tomorrow is not promised nor free from life events that may hinder you from planning well.

Since there are no tomorrow guarantees, I approach estate planning with a good amount of urgency, especially when there are no plans that address incapacity. Make a decision to take action <u>now</u>.

Understand Why Estate Planning is Important to You. You can take action now by understanding why estate planning is important to you and your loved ones. Consider what will be gained if you planned and what will be lost if you don't plan. Acquaint yourself with the pleasure derived from planning, such as peace of mind and confidence, or the pain that follows failure to plan, such as fractured family relationships, a squandered inheritance, or lost family land. If you consider deeply that your authority to plan is derived from God, you more likely will appreciate your responsibility to plan. Any one of these considerations can spur you to take the next step.

Learn What You Don't Know. You can take action by learning some of what you don't know. Research and study why estate planning is important to you. This book, for example, will help you gain more knowledge of estate planning with the hope of moving you forward. Read on! Attend a workshop or seminar presented by an estate planning attorney. A good workshop not only gives you useful insight and information but also motivates you to take action.

Be forewarned, though. Do not confuse your acquired knowledge with the skill needed to prepare a sound estate plan. The art of estate planning requires good counsel.

> **Do not confuse your acquired knowledge with the skill needed to prepare a sound estate plan.**

2. Prepare Yourself by Considering Three Things

Consider your trusted persons. Identify two or more people whom you trust to step into your shoes to make decisions for you if you can't make them. Consider family members, friends, co-workers, church members, and others who have displayed qualities that you trust. It does not matter if you don't feel close enough to ask them to step into your shoes.

While some of you may identify several people whom you can count on, others may draw a blank. Do not be discouraged. Just consider those qualities that you would like to see in a trusted person.

The art of estate planning is identifying and deciding on those trusted persons. In a few cases, your trusted persons may be a professional person or entity. Even in identifying your trusted persons, the perspective of good counsel may be needed.

Consider those you want to benefit from your estate. Sometimes, identifying who you want to benefit is quite straightforward. For example, you may want your spouse and children to benefit. It is so much easier to take the next step when you are certain of the objects of your bounty; however, sometimes the choices are not clear at all. This is where a little more digging and soul searching is needed. Consider what's important to you; the needs you see unmet; the lives you want to influence. Consider the giving that has brought you the most satisfaction. Consider the people or institutions who have influenced your life positively.

Remember, estate planning is an art. As an estate planning attorney, I have guided many clients over the years in leaving their assets to parties that would otherwise have gone overlooked.

Consider your estate. Your estate consists of your property, possessions, and those things you have control over. These are also referred to as your assets. Your obvious assets are your bank and investment accounts, real estate, retirement plan accounts, insurances and annuities, and cars and other tangible, personal property. Debts that are owed to you are also your assets. Consider potential inheritances that can ultimately come into your estate. Other forms of assets are your digital assets — online accounts, photographs, social media, and other accounts stored digitally — which are often omitted in the process of planning.

As important as your material assets are, consider the assets that you can't place a value on. These invaluable assets include your personhood and your right to make decisions about yourself; your values, experiences, goals, and relationships. It's the consideration of these priceless assets that draws an appreciation to the art of estate planning.

Three things to consider:

Your Trusted Ones

Your Beneficiaries

Your Estate

3. Identify the right estate planning attorney for you

Identify your estate planning attorney and schedule an appointment. While identifying your estate planning attorney may seem a daunting task, in today's world, it is not that difficult. Word of mouth referrals is often preferred, especially from those who have used an attorney's services. But if you do not have a referral, never has it been easier to preview your estate planning attorney through internet searches, websites, social media, online reviews, seminars, and speaking engagements.

As you approach selecting your estate planning attorney, rest in this confidence: you are the one planning your estate, not your attorney. You employ your attorney to guide you in exercising your authority to make sound estate planning decisions and to put your decisions in appropriate written form.

In Part III, you'll find an entire section on the importance of good counsel in planning your estate to further guide you in selecting good counsel.

The Art of Estate Planning Is a Process

(Step by Step)

Process comes from the verb proceed, which means to advance or carry on. Process is a continuing development involving many changes; or a particular method of doing something, generally involving several steps or operations.

There is more to estate planning than "I've got mine already done." Planning is an action word. It's a process that has a beginning and continues. Your plan is never complete until successfully executed *after* your death. A plan today may not work tomorrow because of changes in your life, in the people in your life, in the law, in technology, and in business practices. You never stop planning just because you have a plan.

You may have done some preliminary work and selected your estate planning attorney. Let's view the steps involved in successful estate planning.

Law practices differ, so the names of the estate planning steps may not be the same, or the steps may be merged together or spaced out, but the process should be essentially the same. I have selected terms used where I practice.

The Education Step. Experienced counsel knows that an informed client enjoys a more satisfying and successful estate planning outcome. So educating clients is foundational. (I suspect that many estate planning attorneys are teachers at heart.)

Estate planning attorneys will help educate you in several ways: through workshops and seminars, webinars, printed materials, blogs, newsletters, web pages, and in-office consultations. Estate planning attorneys use some or all of these methods to equip you with the knowledge needed to make sound estate planning decisions. In offering this educational component, we as attorneys derive joy from not only benefiting our clients but also the general community.

The Discovery or Initial Meeting Step. Different practices have different names for the first meeting between you and the attorney or the attorney's staff. (Some firms conduct this meeting between you and the firm's paralegal or client coordinator. That arrangement works well too.) Some firms break this meeting into two sessions. You are generally given a questionnaire to complete before or during the meeting.

What's important is that at this meeting you learn the firm's process, fee arrangements, and what is expected of you. Your attorney will learn about you and your history, expectations, relationships, and financial circumstances. Your attorney will generally explore what's important to you and offer recommendations on the type or types of estate plans to consider. Based on your choice, fees are set, and you can then hire or engage your attorney.

Don't believe the fallacy that you don't have enough resources to plan. That's a mistake that too many make, and as a result they never plan. Remember, your most valuable resource is YOU, and you are priceless!

The Design Step. The Design Step involves the deep work of designing your plan, and it is the heart of the planning process. You or counsel may even create a diagram of your plan. The Design Step is where your vision is captured.

Some plans are simple and relatively straightforward, and others are complicated and may take longer to complete. This is the part that I find most stimulating and rewarding for my clients and for me as counsel.

Here's what you will identify during the Design Step:

- **Your Important People and Relationships:** We ask you to identify the important people in your life. These will include your spouse, children and descendants, parents, siblings, close friends, trusted advisors and other relationships, as well as your church, charity, and causes. Identifying this pool of persons and affiliations before you draft your plan helps give shape to your plan decisions.

- *Your Fiduciaries or Trusted People:* Your fiduciaries, the general term for your trusted agents and representatives, include your agent under your powers of attorney, your guardian for minor children, your personal representative under your will, and the trustee of your trust, if you are designing a trust. You will be asked to consider back-up fiduciaries as well.

- *Your Beneficiaries:* These are the people and entities that you want to benefit from your estate during your life and after your death. Most of the planning in this step is for after-death beneficiaries.

o **Your Rules in the Event of Incapacity**: There is a variety of approaches to making decisions about what happens if you become incapacitated, such as delegating authority to your agent to make decisions for you (powers of attorney); instructing your agent on how to make decisions (advance directives), and granting access to medical information (HIPAA authorizations). You also have authority to determine how your income and assets are to be utilized if incapacitated.

- **Your Rules for Administering Your Estate Upon Your Death:** Some of your rules may be standard and general, while other rules may be personalized and instructive. For example, you may give very specific instructions on what happens to your residence and who occupies it immediately after your death. The extent of your rule-making will depend on the tools that you use to transfer your assets at death. We will examine these tools more closely in the chapters that follow.

- **Your Who, What, When, Where, How, and Why Rules:** You may have already decided who gets what, but here you refine *how* your plans are to be carried out. For example:

    - Do you want your beneficiary to receive a specific tangible gift? A specific dollar amount? A percentage of the remaining whole?

- What if the beneficiary predeceases you?

- When is the beneficiary to receive the gift?

- What are the conditions for receiving the gift?

- What are the guidelines for distributing the gift?

- Do you want to include incentive provisions that promote desired behaviors, address specific issues, or encourage the achievement of certain milestones?

- What are the instructions on the use of the gift?

- How much do you want to protect the gift from the beneficiary's creditors, predators, or potential divorcing spouse?

- What happens to the gift upon the death of the beneficiary?

- Are there remote contingency plans if none of your designated beneficiaries are living?

These are some of the considerations that will be addressed during the design phase, especially if you are establishing a trust. Do not feel overwhelmed by the multitude of gifting decisions. Your counsel will gently guide you through these decisions.

- **Your Fiduciary Powers and Plan Administration Rules:** These rules are the design considerations that instruct your fiduciaries on how to administer your plan. These rules are crafted by your planning counsel, and in most cases, without significant input by you. They are what I often refer to as the "under the hood" components of your plan design. When most of us buy a car, we decide the make, model, and overall features of the car. We seldom consider the mechanisms that are underneath the hood of the car. We just want to be assured that the car operates as it is supposed to. Likewise, many of the fiduciary powers and administration rules are mechanisms that are "under the hood" of your trust. Your estate planning counsel will point out what's important for you to weigh in on, but mostly these are predetermined operations.

  - **A Word of Caution:** With that said about the "under the hood" provisions, it is still vital that you review all the terms of your trust and other documents. Raise questions if you must. Your document will become a binding, legal agreement that will be the rule book your trustee or representative must follow.

- **Your Real Legacy:** An important part of planning is considering your real legacy – the aspects of your life lived worth sharing and passing on to others. This is a step that is often overlooked in the design process. Are there values, preferences, remembrances, lessons, words of wisdom and meaning that you want to memorialize in your plan? What a tremendous opportunity to impart in words intangible treasures that are important to you and would be of value to your loved ones.

- **Other Design Considerations:** You may be asked to consider issues related to taxes and your retirement plan, second marriages and blended families, the family home and second home, and plans for your pets, to name a few.

> **What a tremendous opportunity to impart, in words, intangible treasures that are important to you and would be of value to your loved ones.**

The Drafting Step. During this step what you have communicated to your attorney will be put in appropriate written form. You are generally not directly involved in this step of the process.

- **A word about document language and length.** Your estate planning documents are not drafted in everyday, plain English. Many complain about the legalese and length of the documents. There is a good reason for language and length. Legalese is defined as the language of legal documents, which involves specialized words and expressions. This language stands the test of time and legal convention, and although your documents may not be readily understood by you, they are drafted for your benefit. Part of that benefit includes making them readily understandable by the legal community, financial institutions, trust officers, courts, and judges.

    As to the length of your documents, the documents contain many "under the hood" provisions previously discussed. Also, many provisions are included under the theory that it's better to have them and not need them than to need them and not have them.

The Review Step. At this step your attorney will review the draft documents with you. They should be clearly explained so that you understand their effect. Ask as many questions as you need since what you sign will be the expression of your intent. Revisions take place at this step. The ultimate goal is to ensure that you understand and are comfortable with what has been prepared for you, and that they accurately express your intent.

The Signing Step. Once you are satisfied with what has been prepared, you will sign or execute your planning documents. Your signed documents are not merely words on paper, or "paperwork"; they are actually powerful tools that will be used to implement your estate plan. Know them well.

- **A Word of Caution:** Many clients have reported that they felt a sense of relief and peace of mind at signing; however, your work as the estate planner is complete after you take your final breath and not when you sign your planning documents. That's why you should regularly review your plan for changes and updates.

The Asset Alignment Step. In this step, also referred to as "funding" or "asset integration," you ensure that your assets are aligned with your plan. You want to align your assets to accomplish one or more of the following goals:

(1) retitle assets, usually to your trust; (2) strategically designate the appropriate beneficiaries; (3) avoid or minimize probate; and (4) avoid or minimize taxes.

For your trust to work as designed, your designated assets must be owned by the trust either during your lifetime or at death. Titles on real and personal property are changed. Beneficiary designations are made or revised on financial assets, insurance policies, and retirement plans. You may be dealing with a host of different financial institutions, each having their peculiar requirements. If probate avoidance is one of your goals, you will want to be sure that there are no assets remaining in your name at death. This step can be tedious and sometimes frustrating and requires your active participation, but with the guidance of your attorney, it will get done.

Below are a couple of examples of what can go wrong when assets are not properly aligned with the plan.

Debra had a good estate plan. She was a single parent of 14-year-old Joey, who had longstanding emotional issues. She set up a revocable trust for the benefit of Joey that would be managed by his aunt and uncle as trustees until he turned 35. While she retitled both of her real properties to the trust, she never changed the beneficiary on her $500,000 insurance policy from Joey's name to the names of her trustees. Debra died a year later. While the trust owned two valuable properties, the trust had no funds to maintain the properties' expenses. While Joey was underage, his aunt and uncle advanced the expenses out of their own pockets. When Joey turned 18, he received $500,000 from the life insurance policy. He then distanced himself from his aunt and uncle, refused to reimburse them for their financial outlays, and in short order squandered the cash. The properties were subsequently lost to foreclosure and tax sale. Debra's plan failed because her assets did not follow her plan.

Even if you don't include a trust as part of your estate plan, it is vital that you understand how assets pass upon your death so that your intentions are carried out. Here is an example:

Derek's plan was simple, but it was another example of misalignment of assets. Derek's major asset was his $150,000 life insurance policy. He had designated his niece as beneficiary with the verbal understanding that she would use those funds to pay his final expenses and then use the rest for herself and her daughter Emma. Following a family squabble, Derek changed the beneficiary to his great niece Emma, who was six years old at the time of his death. When he died, Derek's body lay in the morgue for weeks because his estate did not have the cash for his funeral and burial, and his next of kin could not immediately raise the money. Because the beneficiary on his policy was a minor, the funds could not be used to pay his final expenses as much as Emma's mother would have been willing to do so.

Finally, here is an example of what can occur before death if assets are not properly aligned with the plan: Mavis was diagnosed as terminally ill and given a few weeks to live. She put her plan in place, providing for those she cared about; named her son as agent on her powers of attorney, and named him as beneficiary upon her death on all of her checking and saving accounts. Mavis lived months longer that her prognosis. Because she could no longer manage her affairs, her son went to the bank with the power of attorney to access her accounts to pay bills. The bank failed to honor the power of attorney on a technical ground, leaving the son with no access to her funds while she was living. Asset alignment, especially where the need to access funds appears imminent, means having the bank recognize the son's agency even before Mavis became incapacitated or retitling the accounts to include the son as co-owner.

No matter how diligent you and your counsel are about retitling property and designating the proper beneficiaries, you should review your assets periodically to ensure alignment with your plan. The concept of asset alignment will become clearer once you understand how assets are transferred at death in the following chapters.

The Review and Continuing Care Step. Once your plan has been signed and the assets have been aligned, you should review your plan at least once every two or three years. Here's why: change is the one constant in life. You change. Your purpose, goals, and vision change. Your fiduciaries change. Your beneficiaries and their needs change. The law and the legal landscape change. Business practices and technology change. In view of constant change, your plan may need to change.

The worst plan is no plan at all. The next worst plan is one that is not maintained because a plan that is not maintained is one that will likely fail.

Your estate planning counsel may offer a paid review plan or a courtesy periodic review. Regardless, my advice is to follow up with regular reviews of your plan, whether you think you need them or not.

Your planning documents are the power tools that implement your estate plan

PART II – THE 7 ESSENTIAL ESTATE PLANNING TOOLS

A tool is defined as a "device or implement... used to carry out a particular function."

www.dictionary.com

There are seven essential tools that you have at your disposal to implement your plan. The first three are:

- o Powers of Attorney
- o Advance Directives
- o HIPAA Authorizations

These three tools are for transferring your decision-making authority during incapacity. We frequently refer to them as "above ground" tools because they are used to implement your plan while you are living. These tools cease their effectiveness upon death.

The following four tools are primarily for transferring your assets upon death. We refer to them as "below ground" tools as they are generally effective after your death to implement your plan of asset transfer.

- Wills and Probate
- Joint Ownership
- Payable on Death Transfers
- Trusts

In addition to the seven essential estate planning tools, we will also look at two other useful tools: lifetime gifting and life estate deeds.

Finally, we will examine how trusts are used in advanced estate planning.

ABOVE GROUND TOOLS

Powers of attorney, advance directives, and HIPAA authorizations are the above ground tools. By using these tools collectively, you empower a trusted person — your agent — to make decisions for you that adhere to how you want to live if you become incapacitated and can no longer make decisions for yourself.

Tool 1 – Powers of Attorney

In the simplest of terms, a power of attorney enables you — the principal — to empower your agent to step into your shoes and make legal, medical, and other decisions for you. Powers of attorney for estate planning purposes fall into two categories: Power of Attorney (POA) for Finances and Personal Decisions and Power of Attorney for Health Care (HCPOA). While the POA and HCPOA can be combined, the better practice is to prepare them as separate documents. We will examine them separately.

Powers of Attorney (POA) for Finances and Personal Decisions

There is almost no limit to the types of transactions and decisions that you can authorize your agent to make for you. You can authorize your agent to access your personal information and financial accounts, pay bills, file your tax returns, sell your property, make investment decisions, and hire and fire professionals. There are some things the law won't allow your agent to do for you, such as marry, divorce, or vote. Nevertheless, given the scope of your agent's authority, you can see that a POA is an extremely powerful tool.

Everyone 18 years and older should have a POA. No legal decision can be made on behalf of anyone over 18 without a POA. This rule applies to parents as well as to spouses. Regardless of the relationship, a POA is required for decision-making by someone other than the principal.

As described in the previous section, if you become incapacitated without a POA, the only recourse is guardianship. Guardianship is a court-controlled process to determine whether you have legal capacity to make your own decisions. If the court finds incapacity, then you become a ward of the state, a guardian is appointed to make decisions for you, and you are stripped of most, if not all, of your rights to self-determination.

Guardianship is an expensive, disempowering, and public process. Guardianships should be avoided. You have the authority to determine who makes decisions for you when you cannot. Use it!

Below you will find more specific information about POAs.

Fundamentals

Scope of Authority. While your POA gives your agent broad authority to act on your behalf, you can limit your agent's authority. For example, you may stipulate that your agent may not sell your residence, borrow money, or make certain decisions on your behalf. The downside to limiting your agent's authority is that if the need arises to act and you can no longer make decisions, your agent's hands may be tied. Consider carefully the limitations you impose and focus carefully on the agent you choose.

Even with broad authority, your agent cannot override your authority to make decisions when you have legal capacity.

POA Content. The vital provisions in a POA are those that designate your agent and those that delineate the powers you give to your agent to use on your behalf. Other provisions can include naming successor agents, determining when your POA becomes effective, giving instructions to your agents, and limiting your agent's powers.

Revocability. You can always revoke or cancel your POA. Just remember to notify whomever your agent dealt with that his authority has been revoked.

When Effective. The best practice is to make your POA effective the date that you sign it. Your agent has the authority to step in and act on your behalf in a crisis if it's effective when you sign it.

The alternative is a "springing POA", which means it springs into effect when a physician certifies that you are incapacitated. Springing POAs are difficult for your agent to use because not only must your agent obtain a medical statement, but she must be prepared to provide updated certifications of your condition each time a transaction is needed.

Remember, you remain in control as long as you have capacity. If you are still uncomfortable with the notion that your agent's authority is effective when signed, then retain possession of your POA. You can also designate a third party, such as your attorney, to hold your POA and release it only when you need your agent to act on your behalf.

When Terminated. Your POA terminates upon your death, if you have not previously revoked it.

Agents

Selecting Your Agent. Topmost, you want to make sure your agent is someone you trust and who is trustworthy. Here are three other traits to look for in selecting your agent: first, choose as your agent someone who will make decisions the way you would make them, and not as the agent would make them. Therefore, choose someone who respects you and your way of doing things. Second, choose someone with the strength of character to stand up for you and to stand up to others on your behalf. Third, choose someone who is humble enough to know when to seek counsel and receive help.

Number of Agents. You can designate more than one agent to serve at a time. Two are better than one *only* if they can serve effectively together. You should always consider alternate agents.

Agent's Responsibility. Your agent is considered a fiduciary – or trusted person - and is responsible for putting your interests above anyone else's, including his own, when acting on your behalf.

Agent's Liability. Your agent is not personally liable for your debt or obligations, and, generally, your agent is not personally liable when acting on your behalf. Your agent may be responsible for paying some bills that get paid out of *your* assets, such as for nursing home care, but your agent would no longer be responsible when the funds run out.

You and Your Agent Acting Together. Even when you have capacity to make your own decisions, you may still choose to have your agent act on your behalf. In that case, you are not giving up your authority to make decisions but are delegating your authority to make certain decisions to your agent. Regardless of your participation in decision-making, you are generally responsible for the decisions that your agent makes for you.

Types of POAs

Statutory POAs. Many states prescribe the powers, language, and content of the POA. These are known as statutory POAs. Whenever a statutory POA is available, you should have one. They are particularly useful in ordinary financial transactions because the statutory POAs are widely accepted and contain commonly recognized powers and terms.

Beware of relying solely on statutory POAs. There are many powers and transactions that they do not cover. For that reason, we recommend signing a more comprehensive or enhanced POA along with your statutory POA.

Also, do not confuse statutory POAs with generically sourced POAs that are found online, in office supply stores, or in form books. Too often the generic forms do not meet the state requirements to be recognized as a POA. You may be lulled into believing you have an effective POA, but it may not work when needed most. Good counsel will help you uncover what you do not know.

Enhanced POAs. A comprehensive or enhanced POA should be considered an accessory to the statutory POA. Most plans require powers that are not covered in the statutory POA. In all cases where there is a need to plan for special needs, asset protection, Veteran's Benefits, or Medicaid, or if advanced planning may ensue, it's best to have an enhanced POA to grant powers to cover those circumstances.

The enhanced POAs include powers that are not commonly provided under statutory POAs, such as the power to make gifts, the power to establish trusts, the power to amend existing trusts, the power to change beneficiaries on accounts, the power to renounce benefits, and the power to disclaim inheritances. There are many more.

You should review the powers with your attorney and make sure you understand their effect.

Practical Considerations

Your Needs. Your POA should take into consideration your circumstances and planning objectives. For a young single adult with no children and few assets, a statutory POA may suit her needs perfectly well. A young adult who is married and has assets may need a more robust POA. Someone who may need an agent to accomplish advanced planning would need an enhanced POA.

Comply with State Law. A POA should comply with state law and practice. Some states have peculiar requirements unrelated to the validity of the POA, and if the requirements are not met, your agent's ability to act for you may be hamstrung. Simply relying on a "do it yourself" form POA may prove disastrous even if it outwardly meets legal requirements.

Instructions to Agents. While POAs confer powers to your agent to act on your behalf, they seldom include instructions on how to exercise those powers. You can include specific instructions in your POA, such as instructing your agent to ensure you remain in your home even if it means there is a greater cost, to provide for other persons, or to consult with other persons before making certain decisions on your behalf.

Acceptance and Enforceability. Your POA is not self-enforcing. That means that an individual or institution is not required to accept your agent merely because he or she has your POA. This can create problems for your agent, especially when your agent is attempting to access funds on your behalf.

Certain banks and financial institutions are notorious for refusing to accept valid POAs. When this occurs, your agent may need to involve an attorney. While some state laws penalize anyone who unreasonably fails to accept a POA, your agent may be required to incur the legal expenses to enforce it. Here is one of many reasons to have your attorney prepare your POA: your attorney will stand behind what he or she has prepared and work toward getting it accepted.

Agencies that Do Not Recognize POAs. You should note that the Office of Personnel Management (OPM), Social Security Administration (SSA), and Veterans Administration (VA) do not recognize POAs as the basis for dealing with your representative. Each of these institutions requires that your representative be approved before it releases money or information. There may be state or local entities that do not recognize POAs as well.

Durable POAs. The word "durable" on POAs means that the POA remains valid even if you become incapacitated. It once had legal significance when POAs were presumed to expire upon incapacity. That presumption no longer holds. So, in most states, POAs, unless otherwise stated, are presumed durable.

Length of POAs. You may wonder why POAs are so lengthy. When I first started practicing law, a one-page POA conferring the agent with general authority was sufficient. Today, the statutory POA is at least seven pages, and the enhanced POA is over 20 pages in length. We live in a complex, transactional, and litigious society. Fraud and the misuse of POAs are rampant. For these reasons, entities and individuals dealing with your agent often require specific language to cover the transaction that they are asked to perform.

A Word on Counsel. POAs are an essential tool in your estate plan. Most powers of attorney have standard provisions. Your attorney may use the same provisions for other clients as she or he uses for you. It's the quality of those provisions that counts. Also, your attorney will know when your power of attorney needs to be updated because of changes in the law, the passage of time, and changes in your circumstances. An attorney-prepared POA may hold greater weight than one prepared from a generic source. Finally, your attorney will stand behind your POA and go to bat for you if your POA is challenged and you no longer have capacity to act. Good counsel will navigate you or your agent through the process.

Health Care Powers of Attorney (HCPOA)

HCPOAs allow you to name someone to make healthcare decisions for you if you are unable to make them yourself. They can be limited or cover all facets of your healthcare. The HCPOA is usually a separate document from the POA.

Unlike POAs for finances and personal decisions, the consequences of not having one are not as severe. Most states have statutes that permit substitute healthcare decision-making, which means if you don't have a HCPOA, there may be an alternative course besides guardianship.

HCPOAs are more readily accepted by healthcare professionals and are not as rigorously scrutinized as are the POAs for finances and personal decisions. HCPOAs are often combined with Advance Directives.

In selecting healthcare agents, select one who is not emotionally driven and can detach from his or her affection for you to make sound decisions based on what you would want. Also consider having one agent serve at a time. It's harder for two or more agents to agree on decisions about your life, health, and possible death.

Tool 2 – Advance Directives and Advance Care Plans

Advance Directives allow you to direct in advance how you want to be treated, be cared for and live. They tend to fall into two categories. The most commonly recognized and used category is Advance Directives for medically related matters. I'll refer to these as ADs. The other category is Advance Directives for non-medical matters. These directives take into account the breadth and depth of how you want to live and be cared for. I'll refer to these directives as Advance Care Plans or ACPs. While this category is often overlooked in most estate planning conversations, ACPs give you the most freedom to exercise your authority.

Advance Directives for Healthcare Decisions

Advance Directives, also known as Living Wills and Healthcare Directives, complement HCPOAs. ADs guide your agent on how to exercise his or her powers under the HCPOA. ADs can include all phases of your healthcare, but they are more often associated with specific types of health circumstances, such as terminal illness, coma, end-stage conditions, removal or use of life support, resuscitation, tube feeding, pain relief, and the use of certain medical protocols. The commonly used ADs address critical and end-of-life circumstances.

The decisions made in preparing your AD have more to do with your personal values and preferences and are less legally driven. Persons skilled in guiding you through this process can be family members, your spiritual advisor, your healthcare professional, a social worker, or your attorney. There are many workbooks and tools to assist you in preparing your AD. Here is where counsel will likely encourage you to seek online sources. Some that we recommend are **www.agingwithdignity.org** (Five Wishes); **www.BegintheConversation.org;** **www.americanbar.org** (Toolkit for Healthcare Advance Planning), and **www.caring.org**. There are sites that focus on specific faith choices in preparing advance directives and care plans, such as **http://www.ChristianLifeResources.com**. Many states have developed optional forms for use in preparing Advance Directives. In Maryland, for example, see the **www.marylandattorneygeneral.gov** site for AD tutorials, information, and forms. There are personal consultants who will work with you in formulating your plan such as those at **www.mjmarkley.com**.

What's significant about HCPOAs and ADs is that you set the standard for your care. Your healthcare choices can be planned in advance. You direct the approach and kind of treatment you would want; and you state whom you want as your healthcare providers and specify where you want to be treated. You dictate who should be consulted in any medical circumstance. You describe the environment of your choice. You specify your dietary requirements. Your planning forward for your care can be broad and specific.

Advance Care Plans (ACPs)

Advance Care Plans, which focus on non-medical decisions, are another form of Advance Directives. Over the past 120 years, the life expectancy of a person has almost doubled. In 1900 it was 48 years. Today it's 81 for women and 76 for men. Medical conditions that were previously deadly are now managed, so it's not just a question of how end-of-life decisions should be made, but a question of how the totality of life decisions should be made if you cannot speak for yourself.

With ACPs, you plan your life forward. You put in writing your choices for how to live if you can no longer fully control your life circumstances. An ACP gives voice to a variety of choices that you may want made. For example, you can express your grooming preferences, where you would like to live, who you want to be around, the circumstances in which you want to engage with family and friends, your outings, your food preferences and dislikes, your interests, hobbies, and activities. Most important to some, you can express your spiritual preferences and describe how you want to be supported spiritually and emotionally. These are just some of the choices you can make in advance for a satisfying life even under compromised health conditions.

Margaret Beads' plan is an example of how you can plan for a full life no matter the circumstances. Margaret at 76 was not married and had no children. Her life had always been full of purpose, passion, and friends, and she wanted to continue on that path for as long as she lived. She prepared a plan for her life even if she could not make decisions for herself directly. She put her beloved niece in charge of her plan and designated her great niece as her backup.

Here are some of the plans she put in place that were carried out during the last four years of her life: Margaret Beads cherished her relationship with the Lord and her daily Bible devotions. When she could no longer read, she directed that friends and family should visit and read Bible passages to her. When they were not around, she listened to recorded Bible passages. Her favorite music, praise and worship, filled her room almost continuously.

All her life Margaret Beads delighted in her handicrafts. As her health declined, she worked on simpler projects to accommodate her changing abilities.

She adored gardening and raising her own fresh fruits and vegetables. When she gave up her home and moved into an assisted living community, she maintained a small garden. When she moved to the nursing home, her final destination, her family provided her with freshly prepared foods and surrounded her with her favorite plants.

She identified the people she was especially fond of and whom she wanted to be around. Her niece reached out to those people and encouraged them to visit and spend time with her. They gladly did.

She disliked what she considered the noise and senseless chatter of television. When Margaret was in intensive care, her niece required that the TV be turned off. She required the same when Margaret was in the nursing home.

Margaret put a comprehensive list of her choices in writing. Because of this, her friends and family were never at a loss for what to do for her.

The last four years of Margaret Beads' life were marked by the need for greater assistance from others to carry out her daily life activities. Yet she lived well, fully engaged, transitioning peacefully in the presence of close family.

Margaret Beads is a fine example of how you can plan, not just for the end of life, but for a full and vibrant life under the severest of health challenges. Margaret examined what was important to her and determined that those things would carry her throughout the rest of her days on Earth. She confronted possible life changes with courage. Her plan was clear. She chose the right people. Because of her plan, she lived a life that was fully satisfying to the end, with the help of others.

My hope is that Margaret Beads' story will give you confidence to plan the best of your life forward, anticipating the help of others. Enjoy the art of estate planning.

Tool 3 – HIPAA Authorizations

Federal and state laws protect the privacy of your health records. The laws are commonly known as HIPAA, the acronym for the Health Insurance Portability and Accountability Act. While these laws are invaluable in our systems of protection, they result in the lockdown of an individual's healthcare information without written authorization. A HIPAA authorization gives access to vital health information to your designated recipients. The person you designate to receive medical information is called a Personal Representative (PR).

Shortly after these laws were enacted, a mass shooting on a college campus illustrated the importance of HIPAA authorizations. Parents of injured students sought to find out their children's conditions. What they found was that the doors to medical information had been cruelly closed. Their "children," many of whom were still covered under their parents' health insurance, were over the age of 18 and without a HIPAA authorization to designate their parents as their PR.

This is something too many parents miss when sending their kids to college – HIPAA authorizations, and let's not forget powers of attorney!

What about the aging parent who has one child accompany them to the doctor, another child handle finances, and other children pitch in when needed? All of the children may need access to the parent's medical information. The child who always meets with the parent's doctor may later want clarification of the doctor's instructions. The child who handles the finances may need to obtain a medical bill. If the parent is hospitalized, all the children may want to call the hospital to check on the parent's status. Without HIPAA authorizations given to each child, none could access the information sought.

A HIPAA Authorization is the one *above ground tool* that can be used after your death. (Remember, POAs and ADs terminate when you die.) Your PR can access medically related information any specified number of months after your death. But this post-death access must be included in your HIPAA Authorization.

Many estate plans are designed to avoid probate. Without the HIPAA Authorization, an executor or personal representative of your estate must be appointed by the probate court to obtain medical records. There are situations where the only reason an estate is probated is to obtain medical records or medical bills. So HIPAA Authorizations can be useful, cost-saving tools even after your death.

A Plan for Living. We have examined the importance of powers of attorney, advance directives, and HIPAA authorizations. Together these tools empower your agents to carry out the rules that you have established. You determine in advance how your finances are managed and who makes personal decisions for you. You set the standard for your healthcare. Most important, you set the standard for your living. Skillful use of your "above ground" tools puts in motion *a plan for living*. That's the art of estate planning!

Another powerful tool employed in your plan for living is a trust. I will address trusts as we examine the tools to transfer your assets at death and their importance in life planning.

BELOW GROUND TOOLS

The second prong of good estate planning is passing on your assets after your death to *whom* you want, *when* you want, *how* you want, and *why* you want. The tools to carry out your plan are referred to as "below ground" tools because they are activated when your remains are below ground. We identified them as:

>Wills and Probate
>Joint Ownership
>Payable on Death Transfers
>Trusts

Tool 4 – Wills and Probate

Wills

Wills are the most widely-known tool for transferring assets after your death. A will essentially names who is in charge of your *probate estate* and who receives your assets. You cannot examine wills as a means of transferring assets at death without considering probate. You will see why as we discuss the key things to know about wills. Using a will as the means to transfer assets at your death allows you to maintain control over your assets until the last possible moment.

Here are nine will essentials:

- **Your Authority.** With a will you exercise your authority to decide who gets your assets at death.

- **Probate and Non-Probate Assets.** The assets that pass under your will are those that are owned by you at death and that do not otherwise pass to another person. These are known as *probate assets*. Here's an example of a probate asset: Mary dies with a bank account in her name only. Her will names Joe as beneficiary. The funds in the bank account pass under her will to Joe as a *probate asset* because the account was still owned by her at death.

Let's look at a *non-probate asset* using Mary's facts above with one exception. Mary designated Opie as the payable on death beneficiary on her account. In this case, the funds pass outside of Mary's will directly to Opie and are *non-probate assets*. Even though Mary's will named Joe as beneficiary, the will has no effect over the assets in her account as they passed to Opie automatically at her death and were no longer owned by her.

- **Personal Representative.** You can name the person who will be responsible for carrying out the terms of your will, manage your estate, and represent your interests after death. Depending on your state, that person is referred to as executor, administrator, or personal representative. We will use the term personal representative or PR for short. Even though you have named your PR in your will, the probate court must approve your will, approve the PR, and appoint the PR to serve. Without the court appointment, the PR named in your will has no authority.

- **Probate.** Only through probate can your will be enforced. That's why you cannot fully understand wills without understanding probate, which we will examine in the next section.

- **Choice of Beneficiary.** You can leave your assets to anyone you choose. You can disinherit blood relatives; however, in most states, you cannot totally or partially disinherit your spouse under your will without your spouse having the right to receive a certain share of your estate, usually the share your spouse would have received if you had died without a will. We will discuss the rights of your surviving spouse in the following section on probate.

  Also, some states require that you provide for your minor children as well.

- **Alternate and Residuary Beneficiary.** In naming a beneficiary under your will, you should always have a beneficiary backup plan. Your backup plan may include an alternate beneficiary for a specific gift if your first-choice beneficiary predeceases you or chooses not to accept your gift. Your backup plan should always include a residuary beneficiary and alternate residuary beneficiary. A residuary beneficiary gets whatever assets are left over or not specifically distributed under your will. If you don't name a residuary beneficiary and you have assets and no beneficiary named, your assets will pass by state law as if you did not have a will. Dying without a will is called intestacy, which will be discussed in the chapter on probate.

Here's an example of alternate and residuary beneficiaries: Mary's will provides for Joe to receive the cash in her bank account if he survives her; she leaves the rest of her estate to Opie. The "rest" is the residuary provision, which addresses assets that don't have a specific beneficiary. Opie is Mary's residuary beneficiary. If Joe dies before Mary, then the bank account goes to Opie. If Mary's will did not name a residuary beneficiary, and Joe had died before Mary, then the bank account would pass to her next of kin as determined by state intestacy law. Mary could have named Sarah, Joe's wife, as alternate beneficiary to the bank account to avoid that result. But the best practice is to always name a residuary beneficiary because invariably your estate may contain assets for which there is no beneficiary.

- **Personal Representative's Bond.** The rule in most states is that whenever a PR is appointed by the court, the PR must post a bond to protect the interests of creditors and beneficiaries if the PR mishandles the estate. To obtain the bond, the PR must usually show that she or he has assets equivalent to the value of the probate estate <u>and</u> is credit worthy. If the PR cannot obtain a bond, then the PR cannot be appointed to serve. To avoid this rule, your will can waive the bond requirement. Most wills do that, as it is standard practice by attorneys to include a clause to waive the bond requirement. So why do I even bother to mention the bond rule when it is waived anyway? The bond requirement is seldom discussed but its effect can be decisive in who will be qualified for appointment as PR in intestate estates (estates without wills) and as guardians in living probate.

- **Necessity of Wills.** Even if all of your assets are transferred outside of probate, you should always have a will. Wills are "standby" tools for transferring unexpected assets such as refunds, overlooked accounts, unclaimed property, and post-death inheritances. There are often post-death issues that only a PR can handle such as asserting or defending claims, obtaining information, waiving rights, and making elections.

- o **Revocation.** You can always revoke or change the terms of your will as long as you have the legal capacity to do so.

Probate

Since wills require probate, it's essential to understand this phenomenon. Probate is a court-controlled process to transfer assets at your death. Through this process the court establishes the validity of your will, appoints your PR, and requires the notification of your creditors and heirs. The process also requires that your probate assets be identified and valued; that creditors be satisfied; that all transactions be accounted for; and that the remaining assets be distributed according to the terms of your will. Below are some basics about probate.

Court Controlled Process. Your will is not self-enforcing. The court must first approve your will before it can be acted upon. The court must then appoint your personal representative (PR) to serve. The court's rules govern the management and distribution of your assets.

Although your PR is responsible for carrying out the terms of your will, your PR must answer to the court and abide by its rules.

Ownership Transfer. Probate is the only way to transfer ownership interest that is in your name at death to the name of your intended beneficiary or heir. This rule does not apply to assets that have a designated beneficiary upon death. In that case the asset will transfer to the designated beneficiary without probate.

Contestability. Persons who have an interest in your estate — your heirs or next of kin and the beneficiaries under your will — can contest or set aside portions of your will through the probate process.

Rights of Surviving Spouse and Minor Children – Exemptions and Allowances. Most states have statutes designed to provide for the surviving spouse and minor children during the probate process. They are usually in the form of exemptions or allowances that the spouse and minor children are entitled to receive prior to payments to creditors and beneficiaries. For example, the surviving spouse may be entitled to up to $40,000 in various exemptions in the District of Columbia. In Maryland the surviving spouse is entitled to up to $10,000 and each unmarried minor child up to $5,000 in family allowances.

Rights of Surviving Spouse – The Elective Share. There are also laws in most states to protect the surviving spouse from receiving less than a *statutory share* of the probate estate. The statutory share is the share your surviving spouse would receive if you left no will. The statutory share is referred to as the *elective share* when applied to a will. If your spouse receives less than the elective share under your will, your spouse can elect to decline benefits under your will and instead receive the elective share of your net probate estate. The exercise of elective share rights can affect your plan.

Here's an example of how the elective share works: James and Mary were married to each other. James had one child, Ben, from his previous marriage. When James died his will provided that 90% of his estate go to Ben and 10% to Mary. Under the laws of her state, Mary was entitled to receive an elective share of one third. After James' will was admitted to probate and within the time allowed by law, Mary filed an election against the will to receive the elective share. As a result of her election Mary received one third instead of 10% and Ben received two thirds instead of 90% of James' net estate.

Over the past decades, assets passing at death are increasingly transferred outside of probate. The traditional elective share law has proven inadequate to protect the surviving spouse from disinheritance if the bulk of the deceased's assets pass outside of probate to someone other than the surviving spouse.

The law is also inadequate to protect a non-spouse beneficiary when the spouse receives substantial benefits outside of the will. In the example of James, Mary, and Ben, Mary is able to elect against the will even though most of the non-probate assets passed to her and were the bulk of James' estate. James' desire to give Ben 90% of the probate estate would have been unfairly defeated.

Augmented Probate. To prevent spousal disinheritance as well as other inequitable results, many states have adopted laws known as *augmented probate*. Maryland is one of the states that has adopted an augmented probate statute. Augmented probate allows the surviving spouse to require that all of the deceased spouse's assets including non-probate assets such as insurance proceeds, payable on death accounts, jointly owned assets, and certain gifts made prior to death, be considered for the purpose of determining the spouse's elective share. The statute is formula-based and prevents inequities to the spouse as well as to other beneficiaries under the will.

The augmented probate statute can upend your estate plan if your spouse is being disinherited or your plan involves certain lifetime gifts including gifts for long-term care planning purposes. For the traditional family estate plan, however, where the surviving spouse receives most of the decedent's assets, the augmented probate statute will have no effect on planning. Your estate planning attorney will advise you on how the law may affect your planning.

Creditor Rights. Your creditors also have an interest in your estate. They can indirectly affect your will plan because they are paid out of your probate estate. If your estate does not have enough to pay creditor claims, then some or all of your beneficiaries are likely to receive a reduced share. If your estate is insolvent, meaning that your estate does not have enough assets to pay all of your creditor claims, then your beneficiaries may not receive anything from your estate. In most states, however, as previously discussed, limited protection is provided to surviving spouses and children in the form of exemptions and allowances.

Intestacy. What happens if you die without a will? If there are probate assets, your estate is still probated. It is called an "intestate estate." The beneficiaries of your estate are your heirs and if you have no heirs then your next of kin. State law defines who your heirs and next of kin are. Generally, your heirs are your spouse and descendants who survive you. If you have both spouse and descendants, the law determines their respective share. Your next of kin are your closest blood relatives after your spouse and descendants. They include your parents, siblings, nieces and nephews, aunts, uncles, and cousins. The law gives an order of priority. Some states provide that if you die leaving a spouse and no children, your surviving parents along with your spouse can inherit your estate. The laws governing heirship and next of kin in an intestate estate are called the laws of descent and distribution.

Your Personal Representative If No Will. State law also determines who has priority to serve as your PR if you die without a will. The priority is based on factors involving the relationship to the deceased. Unless the PR applicant qualifies for a bond, which is usually based on credit worthiness <u>and</u> asset holdings, the applicant will not be appointed PR. In that case, the court will appoint an approved attorney to administer the estate. Remember, since most wills waive the bond, the bond requirement usually does not become an issue.

Same-Sex Marriage. In states that have adopted same-sex marriage laws, such as the District of Columbia and Maryland, the surviving spouse in a same-sex marriage has the same rights as the surviving spouse in a heterosexual marriage.

Other Probate Laws. Other important probate laws to consider are the provisions for notifying heirs or next of kin and creditors; for setting limitation periods for filing claims and contesting wills; for taking inventory of the assets; for producing accounts and approving them, and for the distribution of assets. There are also simplified procedures for estates under a certain dollar amount. These provisions are usually called "small estate" proceedings.

Why Not Probate for Asset Transfers?

While probate is the most widely used process for passing assets at death, there are several reasons that estate planners — that's you — seek to avoid probate as the tool for transferring major assets at death. There are various reasons people might want to avoid probate, some of which are listed below.

Reduced Authority. Remember, you have the authority to determine how your assets are transferred at death. Your authority extends to your choice of tools. With probate, the state's rules govern the disposition of your assets. You have the authority to establish your own rules. With probate, you give up considerable authority to assert your rules.

Expense. Probate is the most expensive way to transfer your assets at death to your intended beneficiaries. Studies show that the costs of probate average between 4% and 7% of the gross value of the probate estate. This average range applies if things go smoothly. Where there are challenges, claims, or litigation, the costs take a higher percentage of the estate. The costs for transfers at death involving joint ownership or beneficiary designations are nominal compared to the costs for probate. The costs of transferring assets in trust, though not nominal, are generally less than probate costs.

Time. With probate, it takes longer for your beneficiary to receive his or her inheritance than any other form of asset transfer. According to one national study, it takes an average of 13 months to two years for a probate estate to close. Those figures are based on routine probate administration where there are no claims, challenges, or litigation.

Creditors Protected Before Beneficiaries. Creditor claims are satisfied through the probate process. In fact, probate is designed to protect the creditors of your estate. While the best course is to not leave debt, other tools, such as joint ownership and payable on death transfers, may allow your estate to bypass creditor claims. The art of estate planning involves understanding your options.

Lack of Privacy. Probate is a public process. Probate records are open to anyone interested. With online court records, anyone anywhere in the world can access those records. Within public view are the identities of beneficiaries and the probate assets. Probate can become the fodder for schemes, scams, and nefarious activities.

More Easily Contested. The probate process makes it easier to contest your will and assert claims against your estate. Why? Because your probate assets are public record and are under the court's control, they become an easily identified, stationary target for anyone who wants to attack them. Many claims against the estate are brought on frivolous grounds with the expectation that they will settle solely to lessen the litigation costs to the estate.

Stress. The demands, costs, delays, and uncertainties of the probate process can be enormously stressful if not painful to your survivors.

While transfer by will allows you to maintain control over your assets up until the time of your death, probate minimizes your authority to pass assets at death with minimal costs, delays, mess, and pain.

The remaining tools allow you to transfer your assets at your death and bypass probate. These are often called probate avoidance tools.

Tool 5 – Joint Ownership

Joint ownership is a tool that allows you to leave assets at death without probate. You co-own your property with others so that upon the death of an owner, the property passes entirely to the surviving owner or owners. The surviving owner(s) automatically acquire(s) interest in the entire property because of the terms of the title deed or the account agreement. This type of co-ownership is also called "joint ownership with rights of survivorship." You will sometimes see it abbreviated on fund accounts as "JTWROS."

We will discuss another form of co-ownership known as tenancy in common at the end of this chapter.

Advantages of Joint Ownership

Transfer by Deed or Agreement. Titling by joint ownership is a simple, inexpensive tool for transferring your assets at death to the surviving co-owner. The transfer will occur by deed or by account agreement executed during lifetime. In either case, when one owner dies, the surviving owner acquires title to the entire property. Generally, no further action need be taken to establish complete ownership by the surviving owner other than providing a death certificate.

Joint Ownership Preferred for Spouses. Joint ownership has been the preferred and practical way of transferring assets upon the death of the first spouse. When the first spouse dies, the surviving spouse inherits everything without probate.

Special Benefit to Spouses. The law protects the jointly held spousal property from the claims of either spouse's creditors. This benefit of joint ownership between spouses is the special spousal ownership protection known as "Tenants by the Entirety" or "T by E." T by E ownership offers asset protection that does not exist for non-married joint owners. For example, Mary and John jointly own property. A creditor sues Mary and obtains a judgment against her. If Mary and John are unmarried, the judgment creditor has the authority to collect out of Mary's share in the property; however, if Mary and John are married and the property is titled as "tenants by the entirety", the property is immune to the creditor's collection efforts. The T by E protection does not apply if the debt is owed by both Mary and John, or the debt is owed to the IRS.

While joint ownership is a very simple and inexpensive tool to pass assets at death that avoids the involvement of probate, you should consider some of the concerns about joint ownership.

Disadvantages of Joint Ownership

Loss of Control over Real Property. Joint ownership means relinquishing sole control over your assets. Loss of control is especially evident when dealing with real property. When you add someone to the title of your real estate, you have made an irrevocable gift of the property. The new owner has an interest in the property that cannot be reversed without the new owner's consent. Neither owner can sell, lease, or mortgage the property without the consent of the other owner regardless of who purchased or maintained the property. Adding someone to the title of your real property is quite simple, but without an agreement, you must go to court to buy out the other owner's interest and regain sole ownership.

To illustrate this point, let us imagine that Mary added her son to the title to her home. She maintained the home and paid the mortgage and all the bills. Several years later, she wanted to downsize and sell her home. Her son, who previously had nothing to do with the property, refused to agree to sell. He even refused to allow her to refinance the property to obtain equity from it. Frustrated, her only course of action was to file suit against her son. After costly litigation and expense, Mary chose to abandon both the lawsuit and her home.

Loss of Control over Financial Accounts. With joint ownership of financial accounts, either owner has the right to withdraw funds. So, when you add someone to your bank or investment account, you run the risk of your co-owner withdrawing all of *your* funds.

Loss of Control over Designating Beneficiaries. Joint ownership also means you have no right to control the ultimate disposition of the property unless you happen to be the sole survivor. Take, for example, Janie and Mark who own property jointly. Janie would like to see her share go to her daughter when she dies, so she names her daughter as beneficiary in her will. If Janie dies before Mark, the property will belong to Mark regardless of Janie's will.

Failure to Plan Probate Avoidance by Surviving Owner. On the flip side of losing control over designating beneficiaries as a joint owner is the failure to plan by the surviving sole owner to avoid probate. Remember, joint ownership will ultimately leave a sole owner, and unless there's a plan, the property will still pass by probate on the death of the surviving owner.

In the example of Janie and Mark as co-owners, if Janie dies first, Mark becomes the sole owner. Unless Mark makes plans to avoid probate of the property upon his death, it will be probated in Mark's estate. So, if you want to avoid all probate over the property, you must make sure you plan.

Creditors and Joint Ownership. Your co-owner's credit can affect your use and enjoyment of your property. This is especially true for real property. For example, if your co-owner has poor credit, your ability to refinance your property is affected. Further, your co-owner's creditors who obtain a judgment can force a sale of your real property or attach your account. This applies only to ownership as joint tenants but not ownership as tenants by the entirety.

Mrs. Rand's home had been in her family for more than a century. It was valuable historic property. To avoid probate and ensure it stayed in the family, Mrs. Rand added her grandson's name to the title. Her grandson stopped paying one of his creditors. The creditor sued and obtained a judgment against him. Mrs. Rand was forced to move from her home when it was sold to collect the grandson's debt out of his one-half share of the property.

Tax Disadvantages. When you purchase property that increases in value and later sell it, you will pay capital gains income tax on the increase in value. Your cost of acquiring the property is regarded as your *basis* in the property. If you give the property away, the new owner or co-owner will assume your basis in the property and will pay tax on the increase when sold. An exception to the rule of capturing increase in value upon sale is when you leave your property to someone at your death. The basis that you had in the property gets reset to the property's value at the time of your death. This is known as a "step up in basis." This and other income tax laws favor the transfer of appreciated property at death rather than by lifetime gift.

Here's an example of how the basis rule works: Joseph purchased land years ago for $40,000. Before his death, he added his son Joe Jr. to title as half joint owner. When Joseph died, the land was sold for a net amount of $440,000. Because monies received on the appreciation in property value are taxable, Joe Jr. will owe roughly $40,000 in taxes to IRS on his half interest (assuming a tax rate of 20%). While his father's share got a "step up in basis" with no taxes due, Joe Jr's share did not get the step up in basis. If Joseph instead had left the land to Joe Jr. in his will or trust, Joe would owe no taxes. So, adding Joe Jr. as joint owner cost Joe Jr. $40,000 in taxes.

Transfer and Recordation Taxes. Many states, including Maryland and the District of Columbia, impose transfer and recordation taxes on real estate based on the value of the property being transferred. The combined taxes on transfers can be as high as 3% of the value transferred. If you are considering using joint ownership of real property as a probate avoidance tool, you should factor in these taxes, which would not be due if the transfer were made at death. Some transfers, such as to certain immediate family members, are exempt from these taxes; but transfers to less immediate- or non-family members are taxed.

To avoid probate, Madeline wanted to add her nephew Edward to her title, giving him a 50% interest. In Madeline's state the combined taxes on the property transfer would be $7,250 or 2.9% of the value transferred. After considering the costs of the transfer, she chose instead to leave the property to her nephew under a revocable living trust. Upon her death, no transfer or recordation taxes would be imposed in transferring the property to her nephew under her trust. And, of course, if she had left the property to her nephew Edward in her will, no transfer or recordation taxes would be imposed

Unintentional Disinheritance. Joint ownership can result in unintentionally disinheriting intended beneficiaries. This is the story of Brian and Agnes' children. Brian and Agnes purchased several acres of property adjacent to water and a wilderness preserve. They built their home there with the intention that it remain in the family for generations. Agnes died unexpectedly. Brian later married Jessica and added her name to the deed as joint owner. Brian died, and Jessica became the sole owner of the property. When Jessica died, Jessica's children from a prior marriage inherited the property. Sadly, Brian and Agnes' children were completely disinherited.

Unintentional Probate for a Minor. Joint ownership with a minor will result in guardianship proceedings or living probate if the minor is the survivor. As a general rule, you should never name a minor as joint owner of your property.

Tenancy in Common – The Other Form of Co-Ownership. Co-ownership of property does not always mean that the co-owners have survivorship rights. Co-owned property where each owner has the right to dispose of his or her share upon death is called tenancy in common, and is the more likely way in which co-owned property is held, especially inherited property. In some states, such as Maryland and the District of Columbia, unless the terms "joint tenancy" or "with rights of survivorship" or "husband and wife" are used in the title deed, the property is presumed owned as tenants in common.

Here is an example of the difference between the two types of co-ownership: Mary, Joseph, and Elizabeth inherited property from their father. They each own a one-third interest, yet there is no mention of joint ownership in the deed. They therefore owned the property as tenants in common. Mary dies leaving her interest to her three children. Mary's three children become co-owners with Joseph and Elizabeth. Had the property been owned by Mary, Joseph, and Elizabeth as joint owners, then when Mary died, only Joseph and Elizabeth would have ownership.

It is interesting to note that with joint ownership the number of owners *decreases* upon the death of an owner. With tenants in common ownership, the number of owners generally *increases* upon the death of an owner. It's sadly troubling that when property is held as tenants in common, family land is often lost to future generations due to tax sales, foreclosures, and neglect. As each co-owner dies, the number of new owners often increases, and control over the land diminishes.

In Summary. Loss of control; possible creditor issues; negative income tax consequences for appreciated property; imposition of transfer and recordation taxes; unintentionally disinheriting beneficiaries; gaps in planning, and the inability to control ultimate disposition of the property are the reasons for careful consideration when deciding whether to use joint ownership as a probate avoidance tool.

Tool 6 – Transfers by Beneficiary Designations

Designating beneficiaries of your assets is another simple and inexpensive tool to transfer your assets upon your death while avoiding probate. Beneficiary-designated transfers are based on an agreement between you and the holder of your assets to pass them at your death directly to the person or persons you name. The proceeds of insurance policies, annuity contracts, and retirement benefits are designed to be passed directly to whomever you designate as beneficiary. You can also designate a beneficiary on your bank, credit union, and investment accounts upon your death. Accounts paid on death to a designated beneficiary are called "payable on death" (POD) accounts and accounts transferred upon death are referred to as "transfer on death" (TOD) accounts. Not all accounts allow for beneficiary designations. Also, some accounts, such as certain retirement accounts, require the spouse to consent to non-spousal designations.

Advantages of Beneficiary Designations

You Maintain Control During Your Life. As with assets that pass by will, you maintain control over the assets while you are alive.

Probate Avoidance Upon Death of Owner. As with assets that pass by joint ownership, probate is avoided. The assets pass automatically by the terms of your agreement unless there is a state or federal law to the contrary.

Beneficiary's Creditors Have No Claim. Unlike joint ownership, your assets are not exposed to your beneficiary's creditors.

You Can Change Designations. Unlike joint ownership, you can revoke or change your beneficiary designation at any time.

Inexpensive to Set Up. Designating beneficiaries on your assets is simple and inexpensive for you to set up. Generally, you can do it yourself either by making a request or by completing a form. If the designated beneficiary is your trust, confirm the designation with your legal counsel.

Inexpensive to Collect upon Your Death. Your beneficiary need only file a claim or proof of your death with the account holder. Typically, access to the funds occurs within days of filing the claim or proof with little or no expense to your beneficiary.

No Negative Income Tax Consequences. Unlike joint ownership transfers on death, beneficiary-designated transfers on death impose no negative impact on income tax liability to your beneficiary.

Beneficiary Designations of Real Property. In some states, such as the District of Columbia, you can transfer your real estate upon death without probate. This is done by "Transfer on Death Deeds" (TODDs). As with other forms of beneficiary designations, the advantages of TODDs are that they are inexpensive to set up, they bypass probate, they are revocable, and they present no negative income tax consequences.

TODDs are state-specific and are a relatively new tool. There is some controversy over their effectiveness. Some title companies refuse to accept TODDs and require that the property be probated to transfer title.

Beneficiary Designations of Motor Vehicles. In some states, such as Maryland, you can designate a transfer on death beneficiary on your vehicle title. This is a useful tool since many probate estates are open solely to transfer title of vehicles to beneficiaries.

Why Not Designate All Assets to Beneficiaries? You may ask why not designate beneficiaries for all assets if beneficiary designations as transfer tools are easy and inexpensive to set up, allow you to maintain control, can be revoked, prevent your beneficiaries' credit issues from becoming your issues, give your beneficiaries quick and easy access to the funds at your death, and present no negative income tax consequences? You are right to ask. Beneficiary designations are great tools for asset transfers at death, but there is one major drawback that we will discuss in the chapter "A Little-Known Truth." But before moving on, we will examine two other tools that, while important, are not necessary to consider in every estate plan.

Additional Tools

Outright Gifts

We are expected to give regularly and generously during our lifetimes; however, giving can also be an estate planning strategy. You certainly avoid probate of assets that are given away before you die, but probate avoidance alone is not a compelling reason to give your assets away.

Here are some of the reasons that you may choose to make outright gifts of your assets before you die:

Avoid Strife and Mess. Give a loved one full control of the asset before you die to avoid conflict, strife, and other challenges.

Income Tax Benefits for Charitable Gifts. Take advantage of the lifetime income tax benefits that come from making substantial gifts to charity.

Estate Tax Benefits. Reduce your estate tax liability. For most Americans, estate taxes are a non-issue. Today, you can leave in excess of $11 million (or $5 million after 2025) without incurring federal estate taxes, but if you expect your estate to be worth more than that, then gifting would be a strategy to avoid leaving your heirs with estate taxes.

Inheritance Tax Benefits. Reduce inheritance tax liability. Maryland is currently one of only six states that imposes an inheritance tax on a beneficiary receiving assets upon death. Making a gift to your beneficiary at least two years before your death can bypass the 10% tax in Maryland.

Asset Protection. Protect your assets from *unforeseen future* creditors. Notice that your creditors have to be unforeseen and in the future at the time of planning. True asset protection, meaning transferring assets to third parties or entities so that creditors with judgments or the bankruptcy court can have no claim to them, should be accomplished by estate planning attorneys experienced in asset protection strategies.

Benefits Eligibility. You can plan to become eligible for certain public benefits such as Medicaid, Supplemental Security Income (SSI), and Veterans Pension by divesting yourself of assets. This planning strategy should only be attempted with counsel experienced in eldercare, disability, or veteran's benefits planning.

Another Word of Caution. What you give away, you may never have access to when needed most.

Life Estate Deeds

Life estate deeds are also among the estate planning attorney's toolkit for transferring title to real estate without giving up full control during your lifetime. These deeds have been around for centuries. Here's how they work: you deed property to another while reserving the right to use, occupy, and enjoy the property during your lifetime. This is called a life estate deed. You, as the person who reserves the life interest in the real estate over your lifetime, are called the *life tenant*. The person who receives the interest in the property after your death is called the *remainderman*. Effectively, the remainderman — your beneficiary — receives all the interest in the property when you die.

Below are some things to know about life estate deeds.

Probate Avoidance. The transfer by life estate deed avoids probate.

The Deed Is Irrevocable. The transfer is irrevocable and cannot be undone without the consent of the remainderman.

You Can Retain Maximum Control. You can specify how much control you choose to retain over the property during your lifetime. If you retain the maximum control, you can sell, transfer, and mortgage the property during your lifetime, but you cannot pass it under your will. This is called a life estate deed with full reservation of powers. Even with this much retained power, it may be commercially difficult to sell or mortgage your life interest in the property without the approval of the remainderman because of title company or lender requirements.

You Can Limit Your Interest: You can create a life estate deed and give up the power to sell, transfer, or mortgage during your lifetime. This is called a life estate deed without the reservation of powers. In some states such as Maryland, this is a useful tool for Medicaid planning in reducing the value of assets because your life estate interest is deemed to be worth zero.

Tax Consequences. There are three tax issues to consider with life estate deeds:

- o **Greater Income Tax Liability during Life.** The sale of life estate deeded property that has appreciated in value can result in greater overall income tax liability than had there been no life estate deed.

- o **Reduced Income Tax Liability after Death.** When the property is sold after your death, the remainderman (your beneficiary) receives a step up in basis and is not responsible for prior gains or appreciation of the property. The tax treatment after death is the same as if the property passed by will or by beneficiary designation.

- o **Loss of Property Tax Exemptions.** In some states such as the District of Columbia, you as the life tenant may lose your property tax exemption.

Next: Previously, I promised to show you why beneficiary designated transfers at death may not be the best estate planning tool for you. The same reason applies to all other forms of transfers at death that we have discussed. So let's take a look at a little-known truth in the next section.

A Little-Known Truth

(The Secret Few Talk About)

All the traditional estate planning tools we have previously discussed — wills and probate, joint ownership, beneficiary designations, gifting, and life estate deeds — require that you give up control at death.

What does that mean? You no longer have control over the assets you leave. Remember, you have the authority to leave your assets *when* you want, *how* you want, and *why* you want. You give up that authority to determine what happens to your assets after you die. The assets you transfer at death pass to your beneficiaries outright and all at once! When you die, your beneficiary's authority begins. Your authority ends. Therefore, you give up your authority to determine *when* your beneficiary can receive the benefits, such as at a certain age; or *how* he receives it, such as in periodic installments; or *why* he receives it, such as to start a business. You give up all authority to protect the assets from the beneficiary's own creditors. This is the secret that few talk about in estate planning.

By retaining control of your assets after your death, you prevent the consequences of transferring assets outright and all at once at your death. Here are just some of the consequences of not retaining control after death to consider:

- Depletion of the family home equity and life savings because of long-term care costs.
- Family lands lost to taxes, foreclosure, and neglect.
- Distress to loved ones caused by sudden wealth.
- Gifts that disrupt life-enhancing services to special needs beneficiaries.
- Unnecessary guardianship.
- Your child's education derailed by spending sprees.
- Your adult child's inheritance enjoyed by your former in-laws.
- Your accumulated wealth depleted in just a few years.
- Children or grandchildren deprived of their inheritance.
- Your wealth in the hands of creditors and predators.
- Squandered inheritances.
- Your spouse's assets exposed to creditor claims and predatory assaults.
- Assets left to unintended beneficiaries.
- Sizeable IRAs and retirement accounts drained by purchases and taxes.
- Missed educational funding opportunities.
- Cherished pets left to shelters and euthanasia.

- Public scrutiny of your estate and your beneficiaries.
- Riches received without values, guidance, or incentives.

These are just some of the pitfalls of leaving your lifetime of accumulation outright and all at once, without safeguards, directions, or restrictions.

You probably want to avoid at least one of these pitfalls, so now let me show you a better way – a tool that allows you to exercise your full authority over your estate and still avoid probate.

Tool 7 – Trusts

Trusts are another probate avoidance tool that can transfer assets at death, but they do far more than that.

There is a tool known as the Swiss Army knife. It's a multi-functional tool that contains several different types of blades, a screwdriver, a can opener, scissors – with all the tools folding into one handle. Some Swiss Army knives have as many as 44 functions. I mention Swiss Army knives because they are known for being useful in almost every situation.

Trusts are like Swiss Army knives. Of all the estate planning tools, trusts are the ones best known for their usefulness in almost any type of estate planning situation. They can handle almost everything.

Here is a list of just *some* of the things trusts can do for you:

- ✓ Avoid probate
- ✓ Manage assets; set standards and rules of use
- ✓ Provide for incapacity
- ✓ Maintain privacy and protect against public scrutiny
- ✓ Protect assets from future creditors
- ✓ Protect assets going to surviving spouses from creditors, predators, and subsequent spouses

- ✓ Protect interest of the children upon subsequent remarriage of parent
- ✓ Protect assets left to beneficiaries from their creditors, predators, and divorcing spouses
- ✓ Minimize estate, inheritance, and income taxes
- ✓ Minimize family conflict
- ✓ Protect interests of children in blended families
- ✓ Set guidelines, encourage desired behaviors, and offer incentives to beneficiaries
- ✓ Provide instructions for the use, maintenance, and disposition of specific assets
- ✓ Control the flow of assets from one beneficiary to another or from one generation to another
- ✓ Provide for underage, incapacitated, and special needs beneficiaries
- ✓ Enable eligibility for public benefits such as SSI, Medicaid, Veterans Pension
- ✓ Protect the family home from dissipation and loss
- ✓ Preserve family rural lands and farmlands
- ✓ Provide for pets
- ✓ Enhance church and charitable giving, along with tax benefits
- ✓ Comply with federal and state laws on transfer of guns and firearms
- ✓ Enable wealth-building inside of certain inherited retirement accounts

- ✓ Provide for change, the unexpected, and the unforeseeable
- ✓ Establish family dynasties

Trust Components

A trust is like a basket that holds your assets along with your rules or instructions. The instructions give the trust the "Swiss Army knife" type of utility for every situation. A trust has five components:

1. **Trustmaker.** The trustmaker is the one who sets up the trust, makes the rules or instructions, and parts with legal title to assets by transferring ownership to the trustee. The trustmaker is also known as the grantor, the settlor, or the trustor.

2. **Trustee.** The trustee is the person who holds legal title to the assets, manages the assets, and distributes them according to the trust agreement. The initial trustee can be you or someone else you name. The successor trustee is the trustee who succeeds the initial trustee. Because the trustee holds legal title, this form of asset management is superior to management by an agent under your power of attorney.

3. **Beneficiary.** The beneficiary is the one who has the right to enjoy or receive the assets.

4. **Trust Agreement.** The trust agreement contains the rules or instructions that govern the terms of use and enjoyment of the trust assets. The trust agreement requires that the trustee follow the instructions that are contained in it.

5. **Trust Assets.** Trust assets are the property that the trustee manages, that the beneficiary enjoys, and that the trust agreement governs. As an individual owns many different types of property, such as cash, jewelry, financial accounts, real property, so does a trust.

Remember Your Authority in Estate Planning: Assets in trust do not have to pass outright and all at once to your beneficiary! With other transfers, once you part with title, you part with control. Trusts on the other hand allow you to part with title, yet still allow you to maintain control. You give instructions to your trustee on how to manage and distribute your assets. You set the standards and impose safeguards and restrictions. Your rules and assets go together. Not only do your rules determine *who* receives *what*, but your rules determine *how, when,* and *why* your beneficiary receives your assets. Long after your death, your rules continue. Even long after your beneficiary's death, your rules continue over the remaining assets.

Trusts serve many functions. Trusts serve a variety of functions in estate planning. One trust can serve many functions. A revocable trust for example can avoid probate; manage assets upon incapacity; preserve privacy; protect your beneficiaries from their creditors, predators, and divorce; provide for generational transfer of assets; and accommodate change, the unexpected and unforeseeable – all while retaining your ability to amend or revoke it. While one trust can serve a variety of functions, many trusts are known for their predominant purpose such as Asset Protection Trusts, Special Needs Trusts, Marital Trusts, Charitable Trusts, Standalone Retirement Trusts, and Pet Trusts. In learning about what trusts can do, you will see an overlap of functions. We will examine trusts as an essential planning tool, explain some of their functions and purposes, and then examine trusts as advanced estate planning tools.

Types of Trusts and Features

For estate planning purposes trusts are characterized as *revocable* or *irrevocable*, *living* or *testamentary*. We will examine each type.

Revocable Trusts: If you are like most people, you don't want to part with title until you must. You want full control and the ability to change your mind, just as you can do with a will. That is what makes revocable trusts so appealing.

Revocable trusts allow you to have your cake and eat it too. Here's how: a trust allows you to part with title along with instructions on what happens to your assets. As trustmaker, you set up the rules. You can also be the trustee who manages the assets. You can be the beneficiary who enjoys the assets as if no trust existed. As trustmaker, you can even retain enough power that you don't have to follow the rules while all other trustees must follow them.

The benefit of a revocable trust is that you provide instructions on what happens to your assets upon incapacity and death. You name your successor trustee. If you become incapacitated, you can select how your incapacity is determined, such as by a panel of loved ones. Upon your death, there is no probate of your trust assets. You have determined who gets what, how, why, and when and have determined how your assets are managed and used. You have determined who enjoys the assets upon the death of a beneficiary. Finally, if you don't like your plan, you can change it for another.

Your revocable trust is the most flexible and advantageous of all estate planning tools. Yet it becomes *irrevocable* upon your death, and in some cases upon your incapacity.

Irrevocable Trusts: These are trusts that cannot be modified except under limited circumstances. Those limited circumstances include: (1) provisions in the trust agreement providing for modification; (2) agreement by all beneficiaries to the modification, and (3) court approval of the modification.

If you are the trustmaker, keep in mind that you cannot change the terms of your irrevocable trust.

Irrevocable trusts that you establish as trustmaker tend to fall into two categories.

1. **Self-settled trusts.** These are trusts that you set up for your benefit. While you part with title and control, you retain some right to enjoy the trust assets. An independent trustee manages the assets and distributes them to you based on decisions made solely by the trustee. These are also called self-settled trusts, spendthrift trusts, or first party trusts. These trusts are used to protect assets in the trust from the claims of unforeseen future creditors or protect assets of trustmakers with special needs who seek public benefits. Always, always consult counsel experienced in asset protection, special needs, or benefits planning in setting up a self-settled trust.

2. **Third Party Trusts.** These are trusts that you set up for the benefit of another. Generally, these trusts are used to benefit persons with special needs who may be entitled to public benefits. They are also used to manage assets for a beneficiary and to protect assets from the beneficiary's creditor, predator, and divorcing spouse claims. As trustmaker, you may or may not serve as trustee depending on the purpose of the trust.

Indirectly, irrevocable trusts benefit you the trustmaker because the assets in trust are protected from your unforeseen future creditors. By removing assets from your estate, you may become eligible to apply for public benefits such as Medicaid and Veterans Pension. Third party irrevocable trusts such as irrevocable life insurance trusts, charitable remainder trusts, and granter retained interest trusts are also used to minimize estate and income taxes.

Another way of characterizing trusts is living trusts versus testamentary trusts.

Living Trusts: Living trusts are established and take effect during the lifetime of the trustmaker. They are also called *inter vivos* trusts. Living trusts can be revocable or irrevocable.

Testamentary Trusts: Testamentary trusts are trusts that are contained in the last will and testament. They take affect after the will-maker's death. The downside to will-based testamentary trusts is that probate is guaranteed.

Testamentary trusts are also established under a revocable trust and take effect after the trustmaker's death.

Examples of testamentary trusts, either will- or trust-based, are marital trusts, beneficiary trusts, special needs trusts, children's trusts, and residence trusts.

Testamentary trusts are always irrevocable.

What You Can Do with Trusts: Essential Planning Solutions

Some planning issues can only be solved by using a trust. Consider the following issues as you are planning your estate.

Plan What Happens If You Become Incapacitated: If you become incapacitated, you have given instructions to your trustee. Some of those instructions include:

1. **Who Decides Your Incapacity.** You can prearrange who determines whether you are incapacitated: traditionally, incapacity has been

determined by a physician; however, obtaining a physician's opinion may be time-consuming, costly, and sometimes difficult. Rather, you can rely on a decision by a panel of your choosing, such as family or close friends. Also, a decision by a panel is a private process and may avoid medical documentation of your condition.

2. **Distribution of Your Assets.** You can prearrange how assets are distributed on your behalf. You can have them distributed to you, to others, or directly to your providers and creditors.

3. **How to Spend on Your Behalf.** You can dictate how to spend assets on your behalf. For example, you may want to remain at home, and direct your trustee to use your assets to support that decision such as paying for caregivers, companion care, adaptive equipment, and spiritual support.

4. **Other Beneficiaries.** You can declare who may benefit from your assets besides yourself, and how that decision is made.

5. **Authorize Advanced Estate Planning.** You decide whether your trustee can engage in further estate planning on your behalf such as planning for long-term care, obtaining public benefits, or minimizing taxes.

Avoid Probate. Because you have parted with title and trust assets are not in your name at your death, there is no need to probate them. Remember, probate deals with assets that are in your name at the time of your death. But watch out for a common mistake of failing to transfer assets to the trust. As a result, either those assets don't get to the intended beneficiary or they must be probated. To avoid probate, your trust must be properly funded with your assets.

Maintain Privacy. Privacy during life and at death are important considerations. Relying exclusively on powers of attorney to manage your affairs can broadcast that you are incapacitated. Probate is a public record of what you leave and to whom. Trusts afford significant privacy. Even your beneficiaries need not know what other beneficiaries receive.

Distribute Assets *When* You Want. Timing of asset distribution is critical. Your death may not be the convenient time for a beneficiary to receive their inheritance. Assets that go to an underage child or legally incapacitated person will often require management by a court-appointed guardian unless held in trust. Regardless of the beneficiary's age or circumstances, you can control when the assets are distributed. Distribution can be timed to age, an event, or the discretion of your trustee.

Distribute Assets *How* You Want. Your beneficiary does not have to receive what you give all at once. Studies show that most inheritances are depleted in three years. Another study involving a luxury car dealership shows that it takes no more than 36 *hours* for a beneficiary to trade his inheritance for a shiny new luxury car! Combine those two statistics, and your beneficiary's inheritance can evaporate in no time. You can avoid these statistics by thoughtful planning. You can direct your trustee to distribute your assets in many ways: in installments; income only (for example, interest and dividends earned on the principal); according to a prescribed standard, such as need or events, or at the discretion of your trustee.

Distribute Assets *Why* You Want. Your giving may be purpose-driven. Such purposes include education; home purchase; business start-up, or incentives to encourage public service, charitable giving, and religious activity. One trustmaker wanted to instill in his children and grandchildren a passion for lifelong learning, and through his trust provided the means to do so. Another trustmaker wanted to ensure that her nieces, her nephews, and their descendants had a jump-start toward college funding. She used her trust as the centerpiece for family members to support and contribute to college funding, thus serving as a legacy to the succeeding generations. This kind of generational legacy planning can be done by ordinary folk with ordinary means.

Protect Assets Going to Your Beneficiaries: Protecting the inheritance you leave from your beneficiary's creditors is one of basic reasons for using trusts to transfer assets. Not only can you use trusts to protect what you have left against the beneficiary's creditors, but you can also protect against loss through divorce as well as loss caused by the beneficiary's own inability to properly manage assets. For these reasons alone, trust planning should be considered.

- o **The Marital Trust:** This trust protects assets you designate for your surviving spouse while at the same time giving your spouse the power to control, manage, and access the assets. Creditors cannot get to the assets. You direct who receives the trust assets after your spouse's death, which is often the children. You can build in protections for your children in the event your spouse remarries. The marital trust, while formerly used for estate tax planning purposes, is an invaluable tool in everyday estate planning for couples, whether they have traditional families, blended families, or multiple marriages.

- **The Adult Child Trust:** Adult children or beneficiaries are the ones who have not matured in managing their lives. It can be heartbreaking to watch an entire lifetime of wealth-building dissipate in the hands of a beneficiary either through squander, addictive behavior, or creditor claims. An inheritance intended to enhance a beneficiary's life may actually undermine the beneficiary spiritually, emotionally, and physically, as well as financially.

- **The $40,000 Term Policy:** I am often asked, "How much assets do you need to consider a trust?" My response is that it is not the size of your estate that matters but who or what in your estate is important for you to protect and preserve. I once represented a client of meagre resources; in fact, she was on public assistance. I agreed to prepare her will and power of attorney for a nominal fee. Her sole asset was a $40,000 term life insurance policy. She had a special needs daughter receiving public benefits and a son on drugs. She wanted both of her children to benefit. When I explained how a trust worked, she appreciated how a trust-based plan using her policy would help her family. She was willing to pay an additional nominal fee for a trust to protect her family.

- **Protect Assets Going to Beneficiaries with Special Needs**: Persons with special needs who are receiving public benefits of any kind are usually limited in the amount of assets they can own. A beneficiary receiving public benefits who receives an inheritance, stands to lose those benefits unless the inheritance is placed in a protective trust. A third-party trust — one that the trustmaker sets up for the beneficiary — is the best kind of protective trust. If there is no third-party trust, the beneficiary stands to lose all public benefits unless he is eligible to establish what is known as a first-party trust. This type of trust is more restrictive than a third-party trust, and requires payback to the government of any unused proceeds when the beneficiary dies or terminates the trust. See the section on Preserve Your Assets if You Become a Person with Special Needs. Third-party trusts should always be considered when leaving assets to a beneficiary with special needs. In fact, because there is always the possibility that a beneficiary may become a person with special needs, special needs trust provisions should be available in every trust.

Leave Your Legacy: Your legacy is something that you leave behind to be remembered by. Your legacy can be far more enduring than money and material things. You can leave wisdom, values, guidance, incentives, messages, reminders, and footprints. These are the legacies that can indelibly mark the lives of those who follow you.

Give to Church, Charity, and Causes: You can benefit your church, charity, or cause with planned giving strategies that can both leverage your giving and reduce taxes for yourself, your estate and your beneficiary. Additionally, your reputation for giving is part of your legacy.

Plan for Your Pets. Sometimes an overlooked aspect of estate planning is making provisions for the continued care of your pets after you become disabled or die. Trusts can ensure that your pets are provided for.

Avoid or Minimize Taxes. Until recently, one of the major uses of trusts, particularly irrevocable trusts, was to avoid or reduce estate taxes. A few years ago, federal estate taxes could consume over 50% of the assets transferred at death. In 2013, the Congress increased the estate tax exemption to over $5 million with the exemption amount increasing periodically. As a result of the exemption increase, over 99% of taxpayers are unaffected by the estate tax. In 2018, the exemption amount was increased to $11.2 million until 2025. While many states also impose an estate tax, most tie their exemption amounts to the federal exemption. Income taxes have now become the new "estate tax" that drives trust planning.

Plan for Change, the Unexpected, and the Unforeseeable. Once a trust is irrevocable, its terms are set in stone. What happens if there is a trustee vacancy and there is no one named in the trust to fill it? What about a trustee who fails in her duties and needs to be removed? What if there is a change in the law that affects trust operation? What if the trust contains errors or ambiguities that need correction? What about a change in circumstances that frustrate the trustmaker's original intent or a change that requires a reformation of the trust? Trust protectors are the solutions to these potential challenges. Trust protectors are individuals or entities that are independent of the trustees or beneficiaries and who function to ensure that the trustmaker's intentions are carried out. Trust protectors can oversee the trustee if called upon to do so. Trust protectors can amend the trust, remove and appoint trustees, resolve disputes, and take other action that would ordinarily be a function of a court. Trust protectors serve an invaluable role in preserving the integrity of a trust as well as minimizing the expense of court litigation. As their name suggests, trust protectors protect the trust. The trustmaker may select his or her own trust protector or leave it for someone else to designate a trust protector if the need arises.

What You Can do with Trusts: Beyond the Essentials

The types of trusts vary with the purpose they are designed to accomplish. As you plan your estate, there may be more advanced planning tools that you will want to consider. Below are several of the common types of trust that are used to accomplish your goals. All of the trusts described below are irrevocable.

Benefits Planning: Preserve Your Assets If You Become a Person with Special Needs. If you need extended care or assistance with your activities of living, our system of laws requires that you pay the costs. As you may know, these costs are staggering. Whether in your home or in a nursing facility, full care costs can average between $7,500 and $14,000 a month depending on where you live, according to the 2018 Cost of Care Survey by Genworth. Preserving your assets thus becomes critical, not just for your future care, but for your family's benefit. This is known as benefits planning, and trusts are significant tools for this purpose. Here are some examples of how they are used:

1. **Special Needs Trusts:** If you are under age 65 and are determined to be permanently and totally disabled, then you can receive certain public benefits such as Medicaid, Supplemental Security Income, and access to benefit programs, provided that you have assets usually $2,000.00 or less and limited income. If your assets are greater than the maximum limit, then federal law allows you to establish a Special Needs Trust to hold the excess assets. The assets of the trust can be used to supplement your care; however, there are strict rules on how those assets can be used. You cannot be trustee of your trust. Furthermore, your trustee is required to pay back government benefits upon your death or termination of the trust.

2. **Medicaid Asset Protection Trusts**: If you are 65 and older, are concerned about long-term costs eroding your assets, and don't have sustainable long-term care insurance, you may consider a Medicaid Asset Protection Trust. This is a significant tool for long-term care planning and asset preservation. Qualifying for long-term care through Medicaid requires that you be impoverished. But you don't have to wait until you become impoverished to have Medicaid as an option for paying for long-term care. The option

becomes available with preplanning so that assets can be preserved for the needs of your family. There is no requirement to pay back government benefits upon your death. To achieve the maximum benefit from this planning tool, planning should be completed at least five years before applying for Medicaid.

3. **Veteran's Benefits Trusts:** If you are either a veteran who served during a period of war or the surviving spouse of a war-time veteran, you may be eligible for VA Pension Benefits to assist with long-term care costs. The most widely used of the pension benefits is known as Aid and Attendance. The VA will pay a veteran up to $2,230 (in 2020) or surviving spouse up to $1,210 (in 2020) in monthly tax-free cash benefits. The benefit imposes income and asset limits. Similar to Medicaid planning, you may elect to preplan using a veteran benefits trust so that your assets can be preserved for the needs of your family. There is also no government payback required. To achieve the maximum benefit from this planning tool, planning should be done at least three years before applying for the pension benefit.

4. **Qualifying Income Trusts:** What if your income is too great to qualify for benefits? Some states, though not Maryland and D.C., allow you to set up trusts to deposit the excess income in order to become eligible for benefits. These are also known as Miller Trusts. As with the Special Needs Trusts, the government must be paid back when the trust terminates.

Protect Assets from Your Own Future, Unforeseeable Creditors: We live in a litigious society, and it's not just the ultra-rich who are targets for lawsuits. Trusts are strategic tools for protecting assets from future, unforeseeable creditors. Under certain circumstances, it is prudent to shield your assets from the reach of potential creditors. There are a lot of laws involved in personal asset protection, and the process can be fraught with traps. Experienced counsel is required.

Here are some things to know about personal asset protection planning:

1. You cannot use this kind of planning to protect assets from known or foreseeable creditors. Any such attempt may violate laws that prohibit transfers that place your assets beyond the reach of existing creditors. These are known as fraudulent conveyance laws. In 18 states (Maryland and the District of Columbia not included) their violation is a crime.

2. With traditional asset protection trusts, you set up the irrevocable trust and give up the right to enjoy and benefit from the asset. However, currently in 16 states you can set up protective trusts and reserve the right to use and enjoy your assets. Domestic Asset Protection Trusts or DAPTs are far more expensive to set up and maintain than traditional irrevocable trusts. Even more expensive are the Offshore Asset Protection Trusts (OAPTs) where your assets are maintained and managed for your benefit in a country with favorable asset protection laws such as Cook Islands and Belize.

3. Plan first from the ground up. Before embarking on protective trust planning, obtain adequate insurance coverage, including umbrella insurance. If you own a business, use the protection of such entities as a corporation or limited liability company. Where practical, take advantage of creditor exemption laws to hold assets, such as those governing homestead rights, tenancy by the entirety (as spouses), retirement plan accounts, and certain types of annuities. After insulating yourself from creditor claims in those fashions, examine your remaining exposure and then you can realistically consider protective trust planning.

Preserve Family Homes, Farms, and Properties: Too often, family homes and lands that are left outright to beneficiaries are lost to taxes, foreclosures, predators, and neglect. Trust planning serves to keep the property intact and protected from the pitfalls of individual or common ownership. Trust planning can also protect your property from being affected by the costs of long-term care. If your intention is to leave your home and other properties to the next generation, make this a part of your planning considerations. It can be done in the context of your general estate planning or on a more advanced level.

Plan for Guns and Firearms: Guns and firearms are a unique category of assets. Federal and many state laws restrict the transfer of certain types of firearms. These laws affect the transfers of firearms not only to your beneficiaries, but also to your agent, personal representative, or trustee. Gun trusts serve to ensure a legal and orderly transfer of these assets.

Build or Replace Wealth with Irrevocable Life Insurance Trusts (ILITs): Life insurance has been used by the financially astute to amass and build wealth during life and across the generations. Traditional estate planners have used irrevocable life insurance trusts or ILITs as tools to minimize estate taxes while providing a source of funds for after-death expenses and acquisitions. Tax law restrictions prevented more expansive use of these tools. Now that estate taxes are no longer the planning focus, estate planners have the freedom to use ILITs for broader purposes. Currently, ILITs are an underutilized and cost-effective tool for asset replacement, for building generational wealth, and for church and charitable giving.

Look into Standalone Retirement Trusts (SRTs): For most families, next to the family home, Individual Retirement Accounts (IRAs) and Qualified Retirement Plans (QRPs) are the largest asset that pass to the next generation.

Until January 1, 2020 a non-spouse beneficiary who inherited a retirement account could defer taxes on the bulk of the account by withdrawing the minimum required distribution over her life expectancy. The account balance could grow and multiply tax-free. This is called the "IRA Stretch Effect" and had been a strategic estate planning tool for building wealth for the next generation beneficiary who may have a life expectancy of 20, 30, or even 50 years. For example, a 20-year-old beneficiary who inherits a $100,000 IRA, by withdrawing the minimum required distributions, could receive $1.7 million over her lifetime while still leaving a healthy nest egg to her beneficiaries. On the other hand, the "IRA Shrink Effect" occurs when the beneficiary decides to withdraw from the account to purchase a luxury new car. The combined costs of the new car and the tax liability on the withdrawn amount can easily shrink the account to almost nothing in less than a year.

The Standalone Retirement Trust is an effective tool to ensure the IRA Stretch while protecting the account from outside influences such as creditors, divorcing spouses, and public benefits requirements, as well as the beneficiary's own inability to manage money.

The **S**etting **E**very **C**ommunity **U**p for **R**etirement **E**nhancement Act, otherwise known as the "Secure Act", became effective on January 1, 2020. The Secure Act eliminated the IRA Stretch Effect for most beneficiaries by reducing the payout period to only ten years instead of over the life expectancy of a beneficiary. The passing of retirement benefits to a younger beneficiary does not have the same wealth-building effect for the beneficiary. The result is that taxes can only be deferred for ten years, which will result in a larger tax bill, Shrink Effect, and a shorter period over which the account can grow tax-free.

The Secure Act allows for the lifetime stretch for disabled and chronically ill individuals and for individuals who are less than ten years younger than the account owner.

The Act provides that the ten-year clock does not start for minor beneficiaries until age 18 or 21, depending on the state.

For the disabled; chronically ill; beneficiaries not younger than the owner by ten years, and for minor beneficiaries, the SRT continues to offer the benefits of tax-free growth and minimal taxes, as well as creditor protection.

Even with the ten-year cap on deferring withdrawals, the SRT still serves as a useful tool for certain beneficiaries.

A spouse who inherits a qualified retirement plan account can continue to take the stretch over his life expectancy by converting the inheritance to his own IRA. Under both the old law and new law, the SRT would have only secondary benefits to the spouse inheritor.

We have identified some of the advanced tools that allow you to exercise your authority in estate planning to the fullest. Experienced counsel can advise you on additional tools including those to minimize estate and other taxes.

In summary, you have explored the essential tools and a couple of others. You see how they work. You have a better understanding of trusts and their many facets and applications. You have also examined some trust planning strategies beyond the basics. So, you now have a handle on the tools used to implement your plan. It's time to move forward in the art of estate planning.

PART III - FINISHING TOUCHES

You now have within your grasp the understanding to create a masterful and meaningful estate plan for you and that will impact the lives of your loved ones. Below are a few additional thoughts to add the finishing touches to your plan.

IMPORTANCE OF GOOD COUNSEL

We were once remodeling our home on a limited budget. One of our major goals was to expand the master bathroom to include a vanity and additional sink. The problem was our idea cost more than we could afford, since it required tearing down a major wall and gutting the bathroom. We were disappointed, unsettled, and about to give up until the contractor casually suggested that we install the vanity and sink *on the other side of the wall*. It was that "Aha" moment where everything fell into place. He offered the perfect solution, at a mere fraction of the cost.

We knew what we wanted. It was our plan for our home, but we could not have accomplished it without the counsel of our contractor. He made his living in construction, had years of experience, and was trained to see *beyond the wall*. I learned a valuable lesson on the vital importance of involving good counsel in our planning.

Good counsel has the vision and insight to see what we can't see. Without the good counsel of our contractor, our plan would have failed.

So it is with estate planning. Your life, family, vision, values, and aspirations make up your estate plan, but good estate planning can rarely be achieved without good counsel. Having good legal counsel is part of the art of estate planning.

Your legal counsel performs estate planning for a living, is trained in the art and technique of planning, and has probably planned hundreds of estates. With your counsel's training and experience, she is ever ready to see *beyond the wall* and help you achieve what appears to be impossible.

Here is what to consider regarding the value of good legal counsel:

The Range of Estate Planning Laws. Do-it-yourselfers beware! Estate planning is not a do-it-yourself project. Did you know that estate planning involves the interplay of more than 20 different areas of law? These areas of law include disability rights, debtor-creditor, elder law, intellectual property, asset protection, real estate, land use, landlord and tenant, social security, Medicaid, Medicare, tax, probate, criminal, family, contracts, trusts, wills, and estates. Do you know which of the areas of law apply to you? Do you know how they relate? Probably not. Your legal counsel is trained to know and guide you in your planning.

Emerging Laws and Trends. New areas of law continue to emerge, such as those involving digital assets. Cryptocurrencies such as Bitcoin have become newly recognized as a medium of exchange. Block chain technology on which cryptocurrencies were built is predicted to alter the shape of finance, social intercourse, and contracts. Even traditional areas of the law are changing. For example, same-sex marriage and parental surrogacy in the age of assisted reproductive technology are radically altering family concepts and laws. Time will tell the extent to which COVID-19 will shape estate planning practices. Already, many states have enacted laws authorizing remote and electronic signing of wills, trusts and other estate planning documents. No matter how much you research and study, no matter what the latest software is offering, no matter what the do-it-yourself pundits advise, there is no substitute for experienced legal counsel assisting you in your planning. To repeat: do not embark on estate planning without the aid of experienced legal counsel.

Failed Plans. Over the years, I have witnessed many plans that fail for lack of good counsel. I have seen plans fail completely where the intended beneficiary gets nothing. I have seen incapacitated individuals unnecessarily become wards of the state under guardianship. I have seen the costs to administer an estate escalate to more than ten times what it should have been. I have seen relationships irreparably torn. I have seen opportunities lost. Regardless of the reasons or the outcomes, the costs from failed plans for lack of good counsel are staggering.

Legal Know-How. Knowledge of the laws involved in estate planning is essential to your plan. Legal knowledge does not come from reading a few books or articles. Legal knowledge comes from rigorous training, study, and application. Good estate counsel possesses the know-how to skillfully apply the law to your situation.

Practical Know-How. Not only does legal knowledge matter, but practical knowledge matters as well. Part of the art of estate planning is knowledge of people, their idiosyncrasies, their behaviors, family and relational dynamics, and what's likely to happen in the face of incapacity, death, or other stressors. Practical know-how also includes knowing "the on-the-ground stuff", or how things really work. This know-how comes from experience and understanding how seemingly unrelated matters affect the outcome of an estate plan. A good example is leaving money to *assist* with college education costs. Without knowing how the Federal

Student Aid program works, your leaving money without a strategic plan could actually harm, rather than benefit, the student's educational funding. Another example is knowing regional practices when it comes to the sale or refinance of an incapacitated person's property by an agent under a power of attorney. Some lenders or title companies may require medical documentation of capacity *at the time* the power of attorney was signed. This proof may be difficult to obtain when needed. It's this type of know-how that good counsel can bring to the table as you plan your estate.

The Do-It-Yourself Danger. The real danger of do-it-yourself planning, or planning without good counsel, is that you won't know that your plan fails until it's too late. It may be too late because of your loss of capacity or too late because of your death. In either case, the toll on you, your family, and your loved ones can be enormous.

You or your loved ones may never recover from a poorly prepared plan because you or your loved ones may never discover its failings until it's too late. That's why good counsel matters.

What to look for in good estate planning counsel? First, you want an attorney whose major practice area is estate planning. An attorney or firm that offers a variety of services, such as negligence, bankruptcy, family law, criminal defense, and wills and trusts, is probably not the best choice for you unless there is an attorney within the practice dedicated to estate planning.

Here are some characteristics that can further guide you: your attorney should be able to easily explain your options, and what to expect step by step from beginning to end of the engagement. Your attorney should be compassionate, be a good listener, and be willing to probe beneath the surface and ask questions. Your attorney should be able to explain concepts to you in understandable terms and demonstrate patience in addressing your questions and concerns. The skills of listening, probing, inquiring, inviting questions, and explaining concepts all allow your attorney to capture the vision for your estate plan. Your attorney should be willing to involve your financial and other trusted advisors in the planning process if you choose.

Many attorneys offer initial meetings without cost. In that meeting, you can better assess if he or she is the attorney for you and your estate planning needs. Even if you have to pay an initial consultation fee, pay it. More than likely, what you learn from that consultation will be worth more than what you paid, especially if you come prepared.

Once you schedule an appointment and meet with your attorney, and after a good exchange of information, ask about fees. You will likely be given fee options based on your objectives and estate planning needs. Many attorneys offer fixed or set fees so you know in advance exactly what you will pay for the plan you select.

Estate planning may cost more than you expect, but with good counsel, it won't cost more than you can afford.

> **Estate planning may cost more than you expect, but with good counsel, it won't cost more than you can afford.**

A Word on Digital Assets

What are your digital assets? They include any information created by or about you electronically and which you can access. Common examples are online accounts, social media accounts, information stored on our computers, cell phones, watches, biometric devices, GPS devices, everyday purchase transactions, and browsing history.

We are fully invested in the digital age without fully understanding its impact on our estates. During most of our waking hours and sleeping hours — think smart watch — we are amassing digital information about ourselves, creating larger and larger digital footprints. These footprints form our digital lives. So pervasive is digital information that we are not able to opt out of creating a digital footprint, no matter how hard we try.

Access to our digital lives has never been more important than it is today. Access is becoming increasingly controlled by passwords and portals, PINs, and authentication codes. While you can access your digital life with some effort, what happens if you can't because of disability or death?

Almost every online service provider requires you to sign its terms of service agreement (TOSA). The TOSA is that lengthy contract you almost never read, but almost always agree to when you download a new program or app. Some of these TOSAs are very specific about what happens upon the death of an account holder and absolutely limit access. Yahoo for example provides that all contents will be deleted upon the death of an owner. Facebook allows you to name someone to access your account after your death. Many other online providers are not so specific. Most do not address what happens upon the disability of the account owner.

Law is catching up with technology. Aside from the limitations imposed by TOSAs, most states now have enacted legislation that require you to give specific written authority to allow access to your digital life. This means that you must include specific written authority in your power of attorney, will, and trust. Under today's laws, simply passing the passwords is no longer an option to giving your loved ones access to your digital life. For them to have access to your digital assets without your written authority is illegal.

Your digital assets often have both monetary and intrinsic or sentimental value. But your digital life may have an even greater value in the future. To understand this future value, consider this: The richest families in the world — Bezos, Gates, Zuckerberg, and others — have acquired their wealth, not from land, oil, finance, or shipping, but from *digital* technology. Presently, your digital life is being monetized, but not by you. In the foreseeable future, you will have control over the monetization of your digital life. Without legal access, your digital life and the assets it contains may be lost entirely.

Leaving Access to Your Information

Your vital information can easily be buried with you. The funeral industry knows this all too well and is a leader in promoting booklets and packages designed to memorialize your biographical and statistical information and final preferences. As important as it is to make available the information needed for completing a death certificate or determining your next of kin or preparing your obituary, it is even more important to provide *access to* your information. The same principle holds true if you lose the ability to communicate information about you during your lifetime.

We have developed a guide to the type of information you should leave access to. It's an encompassing guide that will prove invaluable in the event of incapacity, death, or even a natural disaster. In our office, we have named this guide the "Personal Private Information Profile" (PPIP).

Because the information collected is so personal, specific and private, keep it in a secure and safe place that can be accessed in an emergency. Let trusted loved ones know how to access the PPIP, or even provide a copy to that person as discretion allows. Review and update regularly.

I now consider the PPIP to be among the five most important documents that every adult should have. The other four are Powers of Attorney, Advance Directives/Healthcare Power of Attorney, HIPAA authorizations, and wills.

I encourage you to set aside a day to create your own PPIP, and again, review it regularly.

Personal Private Information Profile

Who

Me: name, also known as & nicknames, address, SS#, home & cell phone #
Family: Parents, spouse, children, siblings -- Family Tree
Support: Church, Friends, Pastor, Doctors, Neighbors, Tax Preparer, Financial Advisor
Others: Employer, Employees, Prior Spouse

Where

Birthplace
Places lived
Schools
Work

What

Assets
Debts
Insurance: life, health, disability, homeowners, auto, long-term care, casualty

Access and Security

Email address and password
Cell phone
Online accounts: Usernames, emails, passwords, personal identification numbers (PINs)
Commonly asked Q&A: e.g., mother's maiden name, high school, etc.

Document Copies

Social Security card
Driver's License or Real ID
Passport
Proof of residency – bills, statements
Birth certificate

Marriage license
Divorce Decree
Death certificate of spouse
Current bank and financial statements
Deeds and Payoff Statement
DD214
Last 3 years' tax returns with attachments or 1099s
Photos of home contents

Final Arrangements
Burial/cremation
Funeral/memorial service
Who/where
Obituary

FINAL THOUGHTS

The art of estate planning begins with you.

You know what good estate planning means. You have the ultimate authority to express plans that can work perfectly for you, your family, and your loved ones. You understand the vital importance of involving good counsel and how to select one. You appreciate the urgency of planning *now*. You are no longer a stranger to the overall process of estate planning. You are more grounded in the essential estate planning tools and how they work. You know more about trusts and how useful they are in planning. You know what barrier may have blocked you from moving forward with planning — lack of skill and knowledge — and you now know how to remove it.

You are now ready to do or renew your plan.

The art of estate planning begins and ends with you.

Much success to you on your rewarding work of art!

The art of estate planning begins and ends with you. It is your estate that you make plans for. In making your plans, you surround yourself with the talent, skill, and counsel of those who can help you formulate your plan consistent with your values, goals, and aspirations.

ABOUT THE AUTHOR

Cheryl Chapman Henderson has been practicing law for over forty years. She is the founder of the Law Office of Cheryl Chapman Henderson, LLC. Her practice is devoted to estate planning, elder law, and probate and trust administration. After graduating from Boston University, she attended George Washington University Law School, where she graduated with honors.

Her career highlights include arguing before the US Supreme Court on behalf of the City of Houston and the State of Texas. She is a sought-after guest speaker, sharing her wealth of knowledge on a variety of legal topics. Mrs. Henderson hosts a twice-monthly workshop and she volunteers her time teaching estate planning to both lay and professional audiences.

Cheryl Chapman Henderson is married to Bishop Lonnie P. Henderson. Together they have two adult children and six grandchildren. She and her husband nurture their union by cooking delicious meals together and tending to their garden. Mrs. Henderson attributes all her success to the goodness of God and continues to build her faith daily.

INDEX

Advance Care Plans, 52
Advance Directives, 27, 37, 39, 50, 52, 60, 135
Asset Alignment, 32
Asset Protection, 46, 78, 91, 104, 118, 126
   Medicaid, 46, 93, 105, 116
   Veteran's Benefits, 46
Authority, 3–5, 7, 9, 10-11, 13, 22, 26, 41-42, 62, 73, 95, 101, 133, 138
Beneficiary, beneficiaries, 26, 27-28, 33, 36, 46, 65, 66, 68, 83, 85-86, 95-96, 98, 101-7, 110, 122
   Beneficiary Designations, 74, 86, 94-95
Capacity, 4, 18, 41, 43, 67, 129
Capital Gains Income Tax, 81
Counsel, 2, 4, 5, 19, 20, 23–36, 46, 49–50, 87, 91, 104, 118, 123, 125–31, 138
Creditor, creditors 28, 66-68, 71, 73-75, 81, 85, 87, 91, 95-96, 98, 102, 104-5, 107, 110-11, 118–19, 122
Digital Assets, 21, 127, 131–33
Domestic Asset Protection Trusts, 119
Drafting, 30–31
Family Homes, Farms, & Properties, 30, 96, 99, 120-21
Family Lands, 85, 96
Fiduciary, 26, 29, 36, 44
Firearms, 99, 120
funding. *See* Asset Alignment
Gift, gifts 27–28, 64, 70, 79, 82, 90-91
Guardianship, 10–16, 40–50, 50–51, 84, 96, 128
Guns. *See* Firearms
Health Care Power(s) of Attorney, 40, 50–51, 52, 53
HIPAA authorizations, 27, 135

HIPAA Authorizations, 58–60
Incapacity, 2, 8, 10–16, 18, 26, 37, 41, 49, 98, 102-3, 106, 128, 134
Individual Retirement Accounts, 121
Intestacy, 65, 66, 71–72
Joint Ownership, 13, 38, 61, 70, 74, 75, 77–85, 87, 95
Legacy, 30, 110, 113
Life Estate Deeds, 91–94
Life Tenant, 91–94
Living Wills. *See* Advance Directives
Medicare, 126
Payable on Death, 70, 75, 86
Personal Private Information Package, 134
Pets, 30, 96, 99, 113
Power(s) of Attorney, 9, 10, 12, 15, 35, 40-50, 100, 129, 133
   Enhanced, 46, 49
   Statutory, 45–46, 49
Probate, 38, 61–78, 80, 83-84, 86-88, 90–92, 95, 97, 98, 102, 103, 106, 108, 126
   Death Probate, 14
   Living Probate, 14–15, 66
Process, 23–36
   Discovery, 24
   Initial Meeting. *See* Discovery
   Review, 23–36
   Signing, 32
Remainderman, 91–94
Retirement Trusts. *See* Standalone Retirement Trusts
Secure Act, 122–23
Self-settled trusts, 104
Standalone Retirement Trusts, 102
Supplemental Security Income, 91, 116
Tax, Taxes, 8, 30, 33, 40, 81–83, 96, 99, 113, 120, 122, 123, 126

Capital Gains, 81
Estate Tax, 90, 99, 105, 110, 113, 120, 123
Income Tax, 82, 85, 90, 93-94, 105, 114
Income Tax, 87, 88, 99
Inheritance Tax, 91, 99
Property Tax, 94
Transfer and Recordation Taxes, 83, 85
Tenancy in Common, 84–85
Tenants by the Entirety, 78
Testamentary Trusts, 106
Transfer on Death Deed, 86, 88
Trust Agreement, 101, 104
Trust Assets, 101
Trust Protector, 114–15
Trust, Trusts, 2, 15, 26, 28, 29, 33, 34, 38, 46, 61, 74, 87, 98-123, 106, 115–23, 126, 130, 133, 138
    Adult Child Trust, 111
    Asset Protection Trusts, 102
    Charitable Trusts, 102
    Gun Trusts, 120
    Income Trusts, 118
    Irrevocable Life Insurance Trusts, 105
    Irrevocable Trusts, 104-5, 113, 114, 119
    Living Trusts, 105
    Marital Trusts, 102, 106, 110
    Medicaid Asset Protection Trusts, 116–17
    Miller Trusts, 118
    Pet Trusts, 102
    Revocable Trusts, 33, 83, 102
    Special Needs Trusts, 102, 106, 116
    Standalone Retirement Trusts, 102, 121–22
    Testamentary, 102
    Third-Party Trusts, 112

Veteran's Benefits Trusts, 117
Trustee, 26, 29, 100, 101, 103, 104-6, 108, 109, 114, 116, 120
Trustmaker, 100, 103-6, 112, 114
Trustmakers With Special Needs, 104
Will, Wills, 17, 26, 38, 61–76, 86, 93-95, 106, 126, 130, 133, 135

www.ingramcontent.com/pod-product-compliance
Lightning Source LLC
Chambersburg PA
CBHW071125240526
45465CB00024B/1178